SPIN Selling

SPIN Selling

Neil Rackham
Huthwaite, Inc.

McGraw-Hill Book Company

New York   St. Louis   San Francisco   Auckland
Bogotá   Hamburg   London   Madrid   Mexico
Milan   Montreal   New Delhi   Panama
Paris   São Paulo   Singapore
Sydney   Tokyo   Toronto

Library of Congress Cataloging-in-Publication Data

Rackham, Neil.
  SPIN selling.

  Includes index.
  1. Selling.   I. Title.
HF5438.25.R34   1988   658.8'5   88–603

SPIN is a registered trademark of Huthwaite, Inc.

30 DOC/DOC   0 3

ISBN 0-07-051113-6

 This book is printed on recycled, acid-free paper containing a minimum of 50% recycled de-inked fiber.

*The editor for this book was Martha Jewettt, the designer was Naomi Auerbach,
and the production supervisor was Richard A. Ausburn. This book was set in
Baskerville. It was composed by the McGraw-Hill Book Company Professional
& Reference Division composition unit.*

Printed and bound by R. R. Donnelley & Sons Company.

Contents

Preface

This is yet another book about how to sell more successfully. So what makes it different from the more than 1000 sales books already published? Two things:

1. It's about the larger sale.   Almost all existing books on selling have used models and methods that were developed in low-value, one-call sales. In the 1920s, E. K. Strong carried out pioneering studies of small sales that introduced such new ideas to selling as features and benefits, closing techniques, objection-handling methods, and open and closed questions. For more than 60 years, these same concepts have been copied, adapted, and refined with the assumption that they should apply to *all* sales. Even the few writers who have tried to give some advice on larger sales have based many of their ideas on these older models. And that's a mistake, because the traditional strategies of how to sell just don't work in the fast-moving and complex environment of today's major sale.

This, I believe, is the first book to take a completely fresh look at larger sales and the skills you need to make them succeed. As you'll see, many of the things that help you in smaller sales will hurt your success as the sale grows larger. Major sales demand a new and different set of skills, and that's what this book is about.

2. It's based on research.   This is the first publication of results from the largest research project ever undertaken in the selling-skills area. My team at Huthwaite analyzed more than 35,000 sales calls, over a period of 12 years, to provide the hard facts on successful selling that you'll read here. There are plenty of *opinions* on how to sell, but a real shortage of well-researched facts. I carried out the research described in this book because I wasn't satisfied with opinions. I wanted *proof*. And now, after a million dollars of research, I can give you well-documented evidence about how to be more successful in larger sales.

I'm writing for those who are serious about selling—who see their selling as a high-level profession needing all the skill and care that go with professionalism in any field. And I'm writing about how to make major sales—that significant business which has the margins and re-wards attractive to high-level sales professionals. In our studies we've worked with top salespeople from more than 20 of the world's leading sales organizations. From watching them in action during major sales, we've been able to find out what makes them so successful. That's the subject of this book.

But how do you know that the methods I'll be describing can help *you* be more effective? I'm confident that they will, and my confidence is based on something more substantial than just hope. When we first discovered the methods described in this book, we weren't sure whether they would help people sell more effectively. For one thing, many of our findings were controversial and directly contradicted most existing sales training; for another, we weren't sure whether the methods used by successful professionals would be too difficult for most people to learn.

So we kept quiet about our findings for 7 years, testing out the practical value of our ideas before we were ready to publish them. During that time we trained several thousand salespeople in the meth-ods we describe here, continuously experimenting to find the best way to turn our theoretical knowledge of sales success into simple and practical methods that could help anyone become more effective in major sales. We measured the productivity gains of the first thousand people we trained, comparing them with control groups from the same companies. The people we'd trained showed an average increase in sales volume of 17 percent more than the control groups. Consequently, I'm confident that this book gives well-tested methods for increasing sales results. It's already helped thousands of people be more successful in larger sales—and it can give the same help to you.

More than 10,000 sales people in 23 countries generously agreed to let Huthwaite researchers travel with them and observe them in action during sales calls. This book is about them and for them with our thanks. Then I must thank upwards of 1000 sales managers who have been part of programs we've run across the world and who have helped refine the ideas I'm presenting here.

Finally, at last count, there were more than 100 people who were closely involved in the research itself and in the development of our ideas. I can't include them all, but special mention must go to Peter Honey and Rose Evison, who worked with us to develop the original behavior-analysis methodology we used in our research. From this methodological base, we were able to produce some initial measurement instruments that let us take the first-ever scientific, quantitative look at sales calls. In those early stages Roger Sugden deserves special mention as the first member of the Huthwaite research team to use these early methods.

For the development of the SPIN Model itself, thanks should go to Simon Bailey and Linda Marsh, who helped during the initial field studies to validate the SPIN Model. Many other Huthwaite colleagues have helped, including Dick Ruff and John Wilson, whose experience as trainers has given me valuable insights into how to express many of the concepts I describe here. Also my thanks to Joan Costich, who helped me revise the manuscript, and to Elaine Ailsworth, who prepared the illustrations.

People outside Huthwaite who have made substantial contributions include Masaaki Imai of the Cambridge Corporation, who has adapted our models to fit the fascinating Japanese sales environment; Jan van den Berg of McKinsey and Co., who has forced me to express these concepts in fewer words than I thought decent; and Harry Gaines, whose instincts for layout and presentation have changed the shape of the book.

Neil Rackham

1
Sales Behavior and Sales Success

The V.P. of Sales met me at O'Hare airport and within minutes we were driving through the Chicago suburbs. He wasted no time in getting down to business. "The reason I want you to do this research," he explained, "is because our sales are about 30 percent lower than they should be. As you know, we're a Fortune 100 company and we invest a lot in recruiting and training. Yet I'm not getting the results I'm looking for. I want your research people to travel with some of my sales reps and find out what's wrong."

This was a perfect opportunity. My organization, Huthwaite, had been working for several years to develop a method called behavior analysis, which allowed us to watch salespeople at work and to figure out which of the sales behaviors they used were the ones most linked to success. I jumped at the chance to try our new methods. Using our research team and some managers from the V.P.'s own organization, we went out in the field to watch how his people behaved in sales calls.

Two months later we were ready to meet with him again to share our findings. In the meeting room, as I stood up to speak to the V.P. and his sales management team I knew he wouldn't like what we were about to say. I decided to take him through the easy bits first, so I said that we'd observed 93 calls and that we'd been out with some of his best performers and with some who were—I searched for a delicate word—well, less than best.

"Yes," he said impatiently. "You don't have to remind me. What did you find?"

I answered cautiously. "Let's first discuss what's going on in the successful sales calls," I suggested, "and see what's different about them. We found..."

"Let me guess," he interrupted. "You went out with some of our superstars. I think I know what's different about their calls. They're good closers. Am I right?"

I hesitated for a moment. "Not exactly," I answered, "at least not if you mean that they use a lot of closing techniques. In fact, in your successful calls we recorded a lot fewer closes than in the calls that failed."

"I find that hard to believe," he protested. "What else did you find?" Before I could reply, a thought struck him. "I guess objection handling could be just as important as closing," he conceded. "Maybe my top people are better at overcoming objections."

Something told me this was going to be a difficult meeting. "Uh, again, not exactly," I answered. "We found that your successful calls contained very few objections. In terms of objection-handling skills, I don't think your top people were any better than your poorer people."

That was clearly the wrong thing to say. One of the sales managers present helpfully tried to get the meeting back on track. "Why don't you tell us what you found about probing skills?" he suggested. "I think that this would be more useful."

The V.P. brightened up noticeably. "Yes," he said, "probing skills are very important. When I'm invited to address sales-training classes, I always stress how essential it is in selling to ask good questions. Lots of open questions—you know, the ones that can't be answered in one word. I tell new people to avoid closed questions and concentrate on asking more of those open questions. I guess *that's* what you found my good people were doing?"

I was cornered and in trouble. With real desperation in my voice, I replied, "You're quite right that good probing skills are important. But from watching your people sell, it doesn't seem to matter whether their questions are open or closed. In fact, your best people aren't any different from your worst in terms of how they use open and closed questions."

The V.P. was indignant. "Are you serious?" he asked incredulously. "Do you realize that you've just taken the three most important areas of selling—closing, objection handling, and probing—and told me they don't matter?" He looked around the table and asked, "Isn't that what this guy's saying?" There was an awkward silence. Finally one of his junior managers spoke, picking his words with care.

"If what he's saying is right," the junior manager began cautiously, "and I must emphasize *if*, then we've been wasting a whole lot of time and money on our sales training. After all, that's exactly what we're training people to do—to uncover needs with open and closed questions, to overcome objections, and to close for the business."

The V.P. thought for a moment. "That's right," he said. "Those are the three key things we teach our salespeople. And not only us—that's what other big corporations teach their people too." He searched his memory. "That's what IBM teaches," he said. "GTE does, Xerox does, AT&T too."

"And Honeywell, and Exxon," added one of his managers.

"I was in Kodak," said another, "and those were the three key things in *their* sales training."

The V.P. turned to me. "I don't want to cast doubt on your research ability," he said, "and I thank you for your efforts. However, I'm sure you'll understand that your findings go against our experience—and the experience of other major corporations—so I've got to believe your conclusions are wrong."

That ended the meeting. As a young and little-known researcher, I didn't have the firepower to challenge the sales-training wisdom of the world's leading companies. I licked my wounds during the flight home, and, being honest about it, had to admit that my evidence wasn't strong enough to be convincing. If I'd been in the V.P.'s shoes, I wouldn't have listened either.

Since that uncomfortable meeting, my colleagues and I have collected much more compelling evidence. We've spent 10 years analyzing over 35,000 sales transactions. We've studied 116 factors that might play some part in sales performance, and we've researched effective selling in 27 countries. Our studies constitute the largest-ever investigation into sales success. Now, having had the benefit of an additional million dollars of systematic research, we could give that V.P. some convincing answers. We could tell him, for example:

- His sales training was fine for low-value sales. What we had discovered was that the traditional selling methods his people were using ceased to work as the sales grew larger. This was why his top people, who were making high-value sales, no longer relied on such techniques as objection handling and closing.

- We now know that there are much more effective techniques that successful people use in major sales. At the time we didn't understand these methods well enough to describe them convincingly, but now we'd be able to tell the V.P. how his top people were using a powerful probing (or investigating) strategy called SPIN and that this, more than any other selling skills, accounted for their success.

What's more, we could also tell him something equally convincing about the companies he listed who were teaching the traditional models of probing with open and closed questions, overcoming objections, and closing. Although neither of us knew it at the time, many of these corporations were becoming distinctly unhappy about the usefulness of this traditional core of selling skills. More than two-thirds of the companies listed during the meeting have come to Huthwaite in the last 5 years to ask us to redesign their major-account sales training. Based on our research into what makes success in the larger sale, we've helped them replace traditional models of how to sell with new and more powerful training.

Success in the Larger Sale

Research has an inconvenient way of coming up with evidence that the researchers sometimes wish they'd never found. That's what happened to me. I was perfectly content with traditional theories of how to sell. When we started our investigations, our aim was to show that classic sales-training methods really worked and had a positive impact on sales success. It was only after we found a consistent failure of sales training to improve results in major sales that we began the long research road that led to the development of the methods described in this book. Before our research, I was happy to think of selling in the traditional terms that our findings now challenge. I was taught—and perhaps you were taught this too—that a sales call consists of some simple and distinct steps:

1. *Opening the call.* The classic theories of selling teach that the most effective method for opening sales calls is to find ways to relate to the buyer's personal interests and to make initial benefit statements. As described in Chapter 7, our research shows that these opening methods may be effective in small sales but that they have a doubtful success record in larger sales.

2. *Investigating needs.* Almost everybody who's been through sales training in the last 60 years has been taught about open and closed questions. These classic questioning methods may work in small sales, but they certainly won't help you in bigger ones. Later in this chapter I'll introduce you to a more effective method of Investigating, which we discovered from the analysis of several thousand successful sales calls and from watching some of the world's top salespeople in action.

3. *Giving benefits.* Once you've uncovered needs, traditional sales training teaches you to give benefits that show how the features of your product or service can be used or can help the customer. Offering benefits in this way can be very successful in the small sale, but in the large one it fails entirely. Chapter 5 introduces a new type of benefit that research shows *is* successful in large sales.

4. *Objection handling.* You've probably been taught that overcoming objections is a vital skill for sales success, and you'll know about the standard objection-handling techniques, such as clarifying the objection and rewording it in a way you can meet. These objection-handling skills are fine when you're making small sales, but in major sales they contribute very little to your sales effectiveness. Successful sellers concentrate on objection prevention, not on objection handling; based on our analysis of how they do it, Chapter 6 describes methods that you can use to cut the number of objections you get from your customers by more than half.

5. *Closing techniques.* The closing techniques that can be effective in smaller accounts will actually *lose* you business as the sales grow larger. Most of the commonly taught closing techniques just don't work for major sales. Chapter 2 describes effective ways of obtaining customer commitment in these sales.

In summary, the traditional selling models, methods, and techniques that most of us have been trained to use work best in small sales. For now, let me define *small* as a sale which can normally be completed in a single call and which involves a low dollar value. Unfortunately, these tried-and-true low-value sales techniques—most of them dating from the 1920s—don't work today in complex high-value sales. The problem with these techniques isn't that they are outdated; people wouldn't still be using them after 60 years unless they had something valid to offer. Their inadequacy, and my reason for this book, is that these techniques work effectively only in very simple low-value sales. Because most writers and training designers have made the inaccurate assumption that what works in a small sale will automatically work in a large one, people have unfortunately come to assume that these traditional techniques are equally valid in major sales, but in this book I'll be showing you that what works in small sales can *hurt* your success as the sales grow larger—and I'll be sharing with you our research findings that have uncovered new and better models for success in large sales.

The Major Sale

I'm writing this book for people whose business is the major sale—and who, like me, have become dissatisfied with the effectiveness of traditional sales models and are looking for something more sophisticated. Many of the major-account salespeople I work with complain that traditional sales training treats them as if they were selling used cars. What's worse, it treats their customers as simpletons waiting to be exploited by verbal trickery and manipulation. Programs of this kind, regrettably, are the rule in most organizations rather than the exception—and their recommendations are a recipe for disaster in major sales. The main purpose of our research has been to replace these simplistic models with ones specially designed for the high-level business interaction that major sales demand.

There's been more written about the definition of major sales than about how to sell successfully once you've defined them. I'm not going to bore you with definitions. I'm sure that whatever the term you use—whether you talk of major-account sales, big-ticket sales, system sales, large accounts, bulk sales, or just "the big ones"—you know a major sale when you meet one.

What I *shall* do is briefly run through some of the characteristics of major sales in terms of customer psychology. It's the changes in customer perceptions and behavior that make major sales different. Let's look at what some of these differences are and how they can affect your selling.

Length of Selling Cycle

Whereas a simple low-value sale can often be completed in one call, a major sale may require many calls spread over a period of months. One of my former classmates selling in the aircraft industry once went 3 years without making a single sale. On the face of it, it sounds like I'm just making the obvious point that major sales take longer. But there's more to it than this. What's really important is that multi-call sales have a completely different psychology from single-call sales. A key factor is that in a single-call sale the buying decision is usually taken then and there with the seller present, but in a multi-call sale the most important discussions and deliberations go on when the seller *isn't* present, during the interval between calls.

Just suppose I'm a brilliant orator who can give a truly compelling product pitch. I'm likely to do well in the single-call sale. This is because the person I'm selling to can be sufficiently impressed by the excellence of my pitch to say yes on the spot and give me an order. But what happens if it's a longer selling cycle, so that I don't take the order immediately after I've made my pitch? How much of what I've said will the customer remember tomorrow after I've gone? Could the customer repeat my smoothly polished presentation to her boss?

Questions like these prompted us to do a small study in an office products company, where we found that less than half of the key points the sellers covered in their product presentations were remembered by customers a week later. What's worse, customers who told us immediately after the presentation that they were likely to buy had lost most of their enthusiasm for the product within a week.

A good product pitch can have a *temporary* effect on a customer, but a few days later it's largely gone. So if you can get a decision on the spot—as you usually can in a one-call sale—then there's no reason why you shouldn't use the temporary effect of a product pitch to raise customer enthusiasm and help you get the business immediately. But woe betide you if you can't get an instant decision. By next week your customers will have forgotten most of what you've said and will have lost their enthusiasm for your product.

Another of our findings, which we'll examine in much more detail in Chapter 6, was that in the one-call sale you could sell by pushing your product, overcoming any objections, and closing hard for the business—but that in a multi-call sale this style was usually dangerously unsuccessful. Why? Perhaps your own experience as a buyer gives the answer. I can remember, for example, going into a car showroom a few months ago. The seller was one of those pushy types who overpopulate the motor trade. After a couple of perfunctory questions, he gave me a really hard sell, using all the classic closes in the book. I wasn't ready to decide, so his pressure was both unwelcome and irritating. After I finally escaped, I made all sorts of solemn vows never to return to that showroom. I'm sure you've had the same kind of experience. Few customers will elect to go back for a repeat dose of pressure. In terms of your own selling, if you pressure a potential customer, then he or she won't want to meet you again. The rule seems to be that it's OK to be pushy if you can take the order there and then, but once you and your customer part company without an order, your pushiness has *reduced* your chance of final success. And because the customer doesn't want to talk with you again, you may never discover where you went wrong. So while a pushy or hard-sell style may work in smaller sales, it generally acts against you when several calls are needed to take the business.

Size of Customer's Commitment

Almost by definition, large purchases involve bigger decisions from the customer, and this alters the psychology of the sale. In a small sale the customer is less conscious of *value*. As the size of the sale increases, successful salespeople must build up the perceived value of their products or services. The building of perceived value is probably the single most important selling skill in larger sales. We've studied it in detail, and several chapters of this book are devoted to how to increase the value of what you offer your customers.

Several years ago we started a study that, because of a reorganization in our client's sales force, was never completed. This is a pity, because it was all about how the need to sell value increases as the sale gets larger. The client, who sold high-cost products, had asked us to advise on whether it was possible to recruit new salespeople whose only previous selling experience had been with cheaper goods. At the point where the project was stopped, we were coming up with some interesting answers. We found that the salespeople who didn't successfully transfer to handling larger sales were those who had difficulty building the customer's perception of value.

I remember meeting one of these less successful people at the Buffalo airport before going out with him to make some calls. He was sitting on a bench with his briefcase open and was surrounded by enough product literature to keep a paper-recycling factory in business for months. He explained, miserably, that he was learning product details because he thought it would help him be more successful. "In my last job," he explained, "I was selling consumer goods and it was my product knowledge that made all the difference." He may have been right, but it was his product knowledge that *prevented* him from being successful an hour later as I watched him fail to convince an office manager to buy a large copying system. The customer was understandably nervous at the thought of spending tens of thousands of dollars. The seller tried to cope with this uncertainty by talking in detail about the product, displaying all his newly acquired product knowledge. It didn't work. The reason why the customer wouldn't buy was that she didn't see enough *value* to justify so large a decision. After all, her present copiers worked relatively well. It was true that there were some reliability problems and that the copy quality wasn't great, but did these justify spending a five-figure sum to put them right? Not on your life—and all the seller's carefully memorized product knowledge couldn't alter the basic fact that his customer didn't perceive value.

How should he have handled the call? Later chapters on the SPIN methods will show in detail how to build increased value in cases such as this. But the message to take now from the call in Buffalo is that what may work well in the smaller sale can act against you in the large ones.

The Ongoing Relationship

Most large sales involve an ongoing relationship with the customer. Partly, this is because major purchases usually require some post-sale support—which means that the buyer and seller must meet one or more times after the sale. Also, the people selling major goods or services usually generate most of their business from developing their existing customers. In contrast, a smaller sale may often be a one-off event where the buyer will never meet the seller again.

How does the length of the relationship affect customer-decision psychology? Perhaps the easiest way to illustrate it is through a personal example. Nowadays, as president of the company, I'm more often doing the buying than the selling. A few weeks ago, as a buyer, I had the perfect illustration of how the ongoing relationship of a large sale can influence decisions. I was involved in two sales on the same day. The first sale was a small one. I needed a new overhead projector for my office, so I had asked a local supplier to send a sales rep to talk with me. The character who appeared was a remarkably unlovely individual who wouldn't have been out of place selling indecent photographs in the back streets of Rio. "It's your lucky day," he began, "I'm sure you can't wait to hear the deal I've got for you!" Actually, what I couldn't wait to do was to get him out of my office. But his price was good, I needed a projector, and I'd never have to see him again. So I cut short his sales pitch, gave him the order, and sent him on his way in 5 minutes flat. From his point of view, it was a successful sale. In most senses it was also successful for me as a buyer. I'd gotten a new projector at a good price—and all it took was 5 sleazy minutes.

Later that day I was involved in a much more significant sale. We were thinking of changing both the hardware and the software of our accounting system. The change would mean a couple of new computers, an integrated suite of accounting software, and 6 months of time to put the whole thing together. I estimated we were talking about at least a $70,000 decision. The seller was a reasonable enough person—perhaps a little shallow and maybe just a bit *too* anxious to do business—but certainly a great improvement on the overhead-projector rep I'd bought from earlier in the day. Nevertheless, as the sales call progressed, I found myself becoming hesitant. As in the overhead-projector sale, the price was good—and I certainly needed a new system—but I was increasingly reluctant to go ahead. "We'll think about it and let you know," I told him. Afterward, when I analyzed what had happened, I realized that my hesitation with the computer system was that I wasn't so much buying a product as entering a relationship. Unlike the case of the overhead projector, where I fervently hoped I'd never have to see the seller again, with the computer I was entering into a decision where I would have to work with the seller over a period of months. And I wasn't certain that I wanted to do this.

What's the moral of the story? Once again it shows that what works in smaller sales may become quite inappropriate as the size of the decision increases. In a small sale it's relatively easy to separate the seller from the product. Although I hated the projector seller, I liked his product enough to buy it. But with the larger decision, seller and product become much harder to separate. Although I liked the computer system, there was no way I could buy it without also buying a relationship with the seller. Because large decisions usually entail an ongoing involvement with the customer, they demand a different selling style. Later chapters will analyze what this difference is and how to use it to build lasting customer relationships.

If you're anything like the major-account salespeople I work with, you'll sometimes feel like a very small cog in a very big and impersonal sales machine. It's often difficult to see that your work has any measurable impact. So it should be comforting to know that, as the sale grows larger, the customer puts *more* emphasis on the salesperson as a factor in the decision. In a large sale, product and seller may become inseparable in the customer's mind.

The Risk of Mistakes

In a small sale, customers can afford to take more risks because the consequences of mistakes are relatively small. In my own case I've a whole closet full of gadgets I've bought that didn't work or weren't half as useful as I imagined they were going to be. Right now, the top shelf contains, among other things, two automatic dialers, a fancy coffee maker, and a clock that speaks the time every hour in an improbable electronic accent. I like to think I'm not the only one who buys useless things from time to time—maybe you've a similar shelf of your own. In all my inappropriate purchases there's been a common factor—nobody else need ever know I've made a mistake. If it was a business decision, I've been able to hide it in my budget somewhere so that even Betty, our eagle-eyed and chronically suspicious budget controller, can't find out.

But it's different with a bigger decision. If I buy the wrong car, I can't put it on a shelf where my wife won't notice it. When I'm looking for a new computer, at least 10 people in my company play some part in the decision, and everybody will use it once it's installed. So if the computer doesn't work, then my whole company knows I made a bad choice. Larger decisions are more public and a bad decision is much more visible.

Customers become more cautious as the decision size increases. Purchase price is one factor that increases caution, but fear of making a public mistake may be even more important. I once had a client in London who cheerfully bought a $40,000 research project from me after just one morning's selling. The decision involved his budget and nobody else's. If the research didn't work out, he had a way to bury the cost so that he would be the only one to know. On the other hand, I had to negotiate much longer and harder with that same individual to get him to spend an additional $1500 in an area where his colleagues would be directly involved.

The Four Stages of a Sales Call

Major sales are significantly different from smaller sales in terms of customer psychology. As a result, they require some very different selling skills. It would be tempting, based on these psychological differences, to go further and to argue that *everything* about the major sale should be unique and different, but this would be just as untrue as the traditional assumption that all sales, whether large or small, require identical skills. However, one of the simplest models of a sales call does seem to be applicable to any size of sale; almost every sales call you can think of, from the simplest to the most sophisticated, goes through four distinct stages (Figure 1.1):

1. *Preliminaries.* These are the warming-up events that occur before the serious selling begins. They include such things as the way you

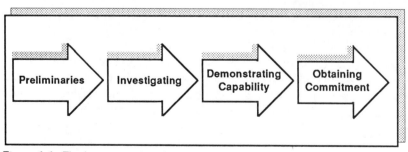

Figure 1.1. The four stages of a sales call.

introduce yourself and how you begin the conversation. Some people believe that the Preliminaries are much more important than the word suggests. I've been confidently told by a number of very successful salespeople that it's during the first 2 minutes of a call that the customer forms crucial initial impressions that will influence the rest of the sale. How important is this initial impact? How much do first impressions count? I'll be sharing with you in Chapter 7 some research that led us to conclude that in larger sales the Preliminaries have less influence on success than we'd first thought.

2. *Investigating.*   Almost every sale involves finding something out by asking questions. You may be uncovering needs or getting a better understanding of your customers and their organizations. As we'll see, this is much more than the simple collection of data. Investigating is the most important of all selling skills, and it's particularly crucial in larger sales. In Appendix A you'll find some case studies which show that the average person in major-account selling can increase overall sales volume by more than 20 percent by developing improved Investigating skills.

3. *Demonstrating Capability.*   In most calls you will need to demonstrate to customers that you've something worthwhile to offer. Most of us in larger sales are selling solutions to customer problems. In the Demonstrating Capability stage of the call, you have to show customers that you have a solution and that it makes a worthwhile contribution to helping solve their problems. Sometimes you demonstrate capability by a formal presentation, sometimes by actually showing your product in action, and sometimes by describing some potential benefits that you could provide. But however you do it, in almost every sales call you must convince your customer that you've something to offer. There are some very effective ways to demonstrate capability in the major sale, but as we'll see in Chapter 5, some of the methods for Demonstrating Capability in smaller sales will no longer work for you as the size of the sale increases.

4. *Obtaining Commitment.*   Finally, a successful sales call will end with some sort of commitment from the customer. In smaller sales the commitment is usually in the form of a purchase, but in larger sales there may be a whole range of other commitments you have to obtain before you reach the order stage. Your call objective may, for example, be to get the customer's agreement to attend a product demonstration, or to test a new material, or to give you access to a higher level of decision maker, and in none of these cases is the commitment an order. Larger sales contain a number of intermediate steps that we call Advances. Each step advances the customer's commitment toward the final decision. It's in this area, unfortunately, that the classic closing tech-

niques taught in most sales-training programs are ineffective and may even hurt your chances of success.

These four stages—Preliminaries, Investigating, Demonstrating Capability, and Obtaining Commitment—are present in almost every sales call. Although this four-stage model is a very simple one, my colleagues and I have found it useful because it has allowed us to break sales calls down into a series of steps that we can study individually. I'll be returning to it throughout the book, using it to provide a structure for explaining some of our research findings.

Of course, the importance of each step will vary with the type of call. I remember once watching a southern banker in Kentucky selling trust services to a customer who looked like Colonel Sanders's twin brother. In this case the Preliminaries took up almost 80 percent of the discussion. Before either party was ready to talk about business, there was a careful "sniffing-out" process that established some of the things essential to doing business in the rural south, such as where you were from, who you knew, and whether your uncle kept horses. Only after an hour of cautious social talk was the customer ready to reveal something of his business needs.

In contrast, I recall the first time I ever went on a sales call in the garment district of New York. There were no chairs in the buyer's office. I assumed this meant that we weren't supposed to stay long enough to sit down. On the wall behind the buyer's desk was a stark notice: "Spit it out and get out." In this call the Preliminaries consisted of "Hello, I'll be brief" from the seller and a grunt from the buyer.

Sometimes the Investigating stage can take up almost the whole call. In selling consulting services, for example, you would have to find out a great deal about the customer's needs before you could determine whether there would be a basis for a business relationship. I've watched an all-day sales call by a management consultant where all but 15 minutes was spent on Investigating. But at the other extreme, I've seen calls where the Investigating stage consisted of just one question, the rest of the call being taken up by an elaborate product demonstration.

So the exact balance of the four stages will depend on the type of call, its purpose, and where it comes in the sales cycle. But most calls *do* include all four stages, even if some of them are very brief.

Which Stage Is Most Important?

Are all four of these stages equally important in ensuring that a call will be successful, or is one more vital than the others? If you judge from the emphasis given it by sales training, by books on selling, or by experienced sales managers, then the Obtaining Commitment stage has to come out as the clear winner in terms of importance.

Let me quote from a sales manager in Rochester who, during our research, wrote me a letter explaining why he thought Obtaining Commitment was the most crucial stage of the call: "The bottom line," he wrote, "is that if you can't close, you can't sell. I'm convinced that most salespeople suffer from being weak closers. If there's one thing I wish my people would do better, it's being able to obtain commitment from the customer by stronger closing." I'm sure that most practicing sales managers would share his view.

The reason why I raise the question about the relative importance of the four call stages is that the answer depends on the size of the sale. In small sales, there's some evidence to suggest that the manager who wrote to me is correct. The people who are good at obtaining commitment—the strong closers, as he would put it—are indeed very successful in smaller sales. In the major sale it's a different story.

The Investigating Stage

Success in the larger sale depends, more than anything else, on how the Investigating stage of the call is handled. We've collected data on Investigating skills from massive studies involving many thousands of sales calls.

Let's begin by reviewing the Investigating stage of the call and why it's so important. Almost every call, I've said, involves Investigating—finding something out from the customer that will enable you to sell more effectively—and to investigate, you must ask questions. Each one of our early studies of selling, in the late 1960s, came up with the same fundamental finding: There were a lot more questions in successful calls, those leading to Orders and Advances, than in those calls which resulted in Continuations and No-sales, which we classified as unsuccessful.

Questions and Success

There's no doubt about it, questions persuade more powerfully than any other form of verbal behavior. And this is not just in selling. Studies of negotiations, management interactions, performance interviews, and group discussions—to name just a few of the areas studied by Huthwaite and other research teams—have all come up with the same basic fact. There is a clear statistical association between the use of questions and the success of the interaction. The more you ask questions, the more successful the interaction is likely to be. And some types of questions are more powerful than others.

Now it's been standard practice in selling to distinguish between two types of questions, open and closed:

- *Closed questions* can be answered with a single word, often "yes" or "no." Typical examples of closed questions would be "Do you make the purchasing decisions?" or "Is your existing business more than 5 years old?" In some training programs these are called directive probes.

- *Open questions* require a longer answer. Typical examples would be "Could you tell me something about your business?" or "Why is that important to you?" Open questions are sometimes called nondirective probes.

This isn't a new concept. E. K. Strong was writing about selling with open and closed questions in 1925, and there's some evidence that the distinction goes back well before then. Most writers during the last 60 years have adopted the distinction between open and closed questions and have generally made the following points about them:

- Open questions are more powerful than closed questions because they get the customer talking and often reveal unexpected information.

- Closed questions are less powerful, although they are useful with certain customer types, such as the garrulous buyer who can't stop talking.

- Even though closed questions are less powerful, you may be forced to use them in certain types of calls—for example, where very little time is available. However, some writers challenge this.

- Open questions are particularly important to success in the larger sale, although closed questions can be successful if the sale is small.

- A general goal of sales training should be to help people ask more open questions.

These conclusions, on the face of it, seem perfectly reasonable and logical. But are they valid? As far as we could tell, nobody had ever scientifically investigated whether call success was influenced by the use of open or closed questions. It seemed an ideal area for some research.

We carried out several studies and were astonished to find that there is no measurable relationship between the use of open questions and success. In one manufacturing company, we tracked 120 calls and found that calls high in closed questions were just as likely to lead to orders and advances. In another study in a high-tech company, we found no differences in the mix of open and closed questions between top and average performers. Some of the best salespeople in this very successful company didn't ask *any* open questions during the calls where they were observed; every one of their questions could be answered with a single word. At the other extreme, several of the top people *only* asked open questions. Some used a mixture of the two. There was no identifiable relationship between success and the use of open or closed questions. We even carried out some studies to find whether successful people tended to start the call with open questions and then move to closed questions as the discussion progressed. We found that some successful salespeople did indeed adopt this pattern. But we also found an equal number of cases where people were successful by starting with closed questions and then moving progressively toward open questions. In other words, none of our studies showed that the classic distinction between open and closed questions has any meaning in high-value sales calls.

Most major companies are spending a fortune teaching people a distinction that—at least in the larger sale—does nothing useful in terms of improving sales results. At a conservative estimate, corporations across the world are spending upwards of a billion dollars a year on sales training that teaches their people an irrelevant questioning technique. Even more incredible, until our little study nobody had ever carried out objective research to discover whether there was any validity in all that was being taught about open and closed questions.

A New Direction

We decided that the focus of our research would be to develop new and positive questioning models that could replace the old ones, which were proving so unsatisfactory. From watching sales calls, it was clear that successful people didn't just ask random questions. There was a distinct pattern in the successful call. If only we could tie this successful pattern down, we'd have a better way to think about Investigating than the seemingly irrelevant distinction between open and closed questions.

As you'll see in the following chapters, we found that questions in the successful call tend to fall into a sequence we call SPIN. In summary, the SPIN sequence of questions is:

1. *Situation Questions.* At the start of the call, successful people tend to ask data-gathering questions about facts and background. Typical Situation Questions would be "How long have you had your present equipment?" or "Could you tell me about your company's growth plans?" Although Situation Questions have an important fact-finding role, successful people don't overuse them because too many can bore or irritate the buyer.

2. *Problem Questions.* Once sufficient information has been established about the buyer's situation, successful people tend to move to a second type of question. They ask, for example, "Is this operation difficult to perform?" or "Are you worried about the quality you get from your old machine?" Questions like these, which we call Problem Questions, explore problems, difficulties, and dissatisfactions in areas where the seller's product can help. Inexperienced people generally don't ask enough Problem Questions.

3. *Implication Questions.* In smaller sales, sellers can be very successful if they just know how to ask good Situation and Problem Questions. In larger sales this is not enough; successful people need to ask a third type of question. This third type is more complex and sophisticated. It's called an Implication Question, and typical examples would be "How will this problem affect your future profitability?" or "What effect does this reject rate have on customer satisfaction?" Implication Questions take a customer problem and explore its effects or consequences. As we'll see, by asking Implication Questions successful people help the customer understand a problem's seriousness or urgency. Implication Questions are particularly important in large sales, and even very experienced salespeople rarely ask them well. We'll be giving a lot of attention to Implication Questions in this book.

4. *Need-payoff Questions.* Finally, we found that very successful salespeople ask a fourth type of question during the Investigating stage. It's called a Need-payoff Question, and typical examples would be "Would it be useful to speed this operation by 10 percent?" or "If we could improve the quality of this operation, how would that help you?" Need-payoff Questions have several uses, as we'll see in Chapter 4. For now, perhaps the most important one is that they get the customer to tell *you* the benefits that your solution could offer. Need-payoff Questions have a very strong relationship to sales success. It's been common, in our studies, to find that top performers ask more than 10 times as many Need-payoff Questions per call as do average performers.

The SPIN Model

These four types of questions—Situation, Problem, Implication, and Need-payoff—form a powerful questioning sequence that successful people use during the all-important Investigating stage of the call. I must emphasize that it's not a rigid sequence. Top people don't ask all their Situation Questions before moving on to Problem Questions, for example. But it would generally be true that Situation Questions are mostly asked early in the call and that the other questions broadly follow in the S-P-I-N sequence.

In this book I'll be looking closely at these SPIN questions and showing you ways to use them to improve your success in major sales. I'll be drawing on Huthwaite's research studies, but even more, I'll be using the experience of my training colleagues, Dick Ruff and John Wilson, who have designed programs that have helped tens of thousands of major-account salespeople from Fortune 500 companies to improve their selling skills and their sales performance. The SPIN questions work because they are derived from watching successful people in action. We hope that, like thousands before you, you'll find SPIN a very practical sales tool.

2
Obtaining Commitment: Closing the Sale

The Huthwaite research shows that success in the major sale depends, more than anything else, on how the Investigating stage of the call is handled. But not everybody would agree with this conclusion. For many writers, Obtaining Commitment is the most important step of a successful sale. When we were beginning our research, not knowing where to start, I approached a number of experts for advice. These people—writers, trainers, and experienced sales managers—generally suggested that we should start with Obtaining Commitment, or closing, as they generally called it. Closing, they told us, was the stage of the sale where the most crucial elements of success would be found, so that's where we should begin our research. I was particularly impressed by this consensus on closing, because these experts didn't seem to agree about very much else. Consequently, our first research studies centered on closing, with the objective of finding which closing techniques were most effective in the larger sale.

Like all researchers, I began by reading, looking for some useful clues to guide our investigations. I spent a couple of weeks in the library searching for all I could find about closing the sale. I plowed through more than 300 references. Every book on selling had at least one chapter on closing. Some, like "101 Sure Fire Ways To Irresistibly Close *Any* Sale," had, as the author so modestly put it, "a lifetime's experience of closing success packed into a mere three hours of reading."

I was fascinated. Here were magic answers to the problems of generating business. The closes I read about included the good old standard techniques that every seller knows, such as:

Assumptive closes.   Assuming that the sale has already been made, one asks, for example, "Where would you like it delivered?" before the customer has agreed to buy.

Alternative closes.   One asks, for example, "Would you prefer delivery on Tuesday or Thursday?"—again before the customer has made a purchasing decision.

Standing-room-only closes.   One says, for example, "If you can't make a decision right now, I'll have to offer it to another customer who's pressing to buy it."

Last-chance closes.   One says, for example, "The price goes up next week, so unless you buy now,..."

Order-blank closes.   One fills in the customer's answers on an order form, even though the buyer has not indicated a willingness to make a buying decision.

In addition to these bread-and-butter techniques, I found a whole encyclopedia of more exotic closes, such as the Sharp Angle, Ben Franklin, Puppy Dog, Colombo, and Double-reverse Whammo. My initial research uncovered literally hundreds of closes, and in the intervening years I'm sure that new closes have continued to appear with impressive regularity. Just last month I was reading an airline magazine that mentioned the Banana Close—a new one for me—and on the same day my junk mail contained a hard-to-resist invitation to learn more about the Half-open Close—a hidden secret of sales success that I'd somehow missed.

No other area of selling skill is as popular as closing. This is true however you measure it, whether by number of words written, number of instructional hours, or number of feet of training films endured by each new generation of salespeople. I was once told by a leading editor that he wouldn't publish any book on selling unless it had the word *closing* in the title. In surveys of sales managers, asking them what skill they would most like to increase in their people, closing has always emerged a clear winner. So there seems to be widespread support for the old selling proverb, "The ABC of selling is Always Be Closing." In this chapter I'm going to be asking:

■ How many of these closing techniques actually work?

- In larger sales, how do such factors as price and buyer sophistication influence the success of closing?

What Is Closing?

Unfortunately, very few of the writers who have so persuasively filled volumes on how to close have defined the term *closing*. Crissy and Kaplan wrote a number of articles in the 1960s where they called it "the tactics used by the salesman to induce purchase or acceptance of the proposition." As a researcher, I find this definition too broad. At Huthwaite we needed a more limited, and more precise, way to define a closing behavior, so in our studies we defined *closing* as:

A behavior used by the seller which implies or invites a commitment, so that the buyer's next statement accepts or denies commitment.

In more digestible English, a *close* is anything that puts the customer in a position involving some kind of commitment. This definition covers the whole spectrum from simply "asking for the order" to using the wildly complex "12-step staircase" technique.

The Consensus on Closing

Closing is a fertile area for sales gurus. Before I review Huthwaite's studies, let me introduce some of the points that other experts have made.

J. Douglas Edwards, called by his disciples "the father of closing," suggests that, on average, successful sellers close on their fifth attempt and that the more closing techniques they use, the more successful they are likely to be.

Alan Schoonmaker is even more specific about the success of closing. He, too, claims that research shows that successful sellers close more often and use more types of closes. And like J. Douglas Edwards, he favors the magic number 5, saying that "you haven't done your job if you quit without asking for the order at least five times." I paid particular attention to Schoonmaker because, at the time, I was developing a training program on the larger sale for IBM and I knew that he was working on a similar program for one of IBM's competitors.

P. Lund, in his book *Compelling Selling*, advises you to close whenever possible—"even when you're miles away from the order." Another popular writer, Mauser, is more restrained, advising you to have a considerable number of closing techniques at your disposal so that if one fails, another can be used "until it is hoped one eventually hits the mark."

I could go on, but I think I've made the point. The consensus among writers on selling seems to be this:

- Closing techniques are strongly related to success.
- You should use many types of closes.
- You should close frequently during the call.

Starting the Research

I started my research into closing in the late 1960s. At the time I was still a university researcher, and the only thing I knew about selling was that it was an interaction between people where money changed hands—and so I reckoned I should be able to find companies who would give me research funds to find out how to make that money change hands more quickly. I was right. Large multinational companies *were* interested and I got my funds.

Talking with Salespeople

My next step was to meet with as many salespeople as possible. I spent a lot of time in branch offices, meetings, and informal gatherings just listening to people talking about selling. I was surprised how often, and how enthusiastically, the conversation turned to closing techniques: "I heard a good close the other day," they'd say, or "Have you tried the Gelignite Close?" or "You know the old 'my pen or yours?' routine? Well, last week...." I was convinced that a good indication of the usefulness of a sales technique would be whether salespeople talked about it on their own time. By this measure, closing was certainly emerging as a winner.

But that's not all: at about this time I was involved in an evaluation study of some training programs being run for experienced sellers. I questioned participants and found something that further convinced me that closing might well be the most important of all selling skills. The average participant could list *four* different closing techniques but was unable to give more than one technique for opening the sale or for handling objections. Less than half of the people I questioned could specify a single technique for investigating customer needs beyond just "asking questions." The group seemed to know more about closing than about everything else in selling added together.

Closing for Real

Talking to other people certainly influenced my opinions. But there's nothing so powerful as a real-life personal experience—which was what finally convinced me that closing is by far the most important of all selling skills. I had left my safe university job and had set up the Huthwaite organization. Now, I realized, selling wasn't just an academic study for me. I had to sell my services or go hungry. So I enrolled in a sales-training program—and paid particular attention to the area of closing techniques.

In the week following the program, I had an appointment with a potential client with whom I'd been talking for several months in an attempt to sell this client a research project. I decided to try an Alternative Close. I'll never forget the result. "Would you prefer the project to begin in September or in November?" I asked, a little nervously. "Let's start in September," my client answered—and I'd gotten my first big sale. I was delighted. I said the magic words and was rewarded with an order. I doubt if even J. Douglas Edwards, the father of closing, could have been more enthusiastic about closing than I was at that moment. For more than a year after my first success, I closed the hell out of everyone. I now realize that I probably cost myself and my company a lot of lost business during that year. But at the time I was a totally convinced hard closer. After all, my personal experience showed that using an Alternative Close had given me my first big piece of business. I *knew* closing worked.

I look back on my enthusiasm for closing with real embarrassment. From what I now know about success in the larger sale, I see closing techniques as both ineffective and dangerous. I've evidence that they lose much more business than they gain. What made me turn against methods that seemed so important to my own success? The rest of this chapter describes the series of studies that finally convinced me that traditional closing techniques have no place in larger sales.

Initial Research

We started our research at Huthwaite with the clear expectation that we would find a strong positive link between the number of times a seller closed and whether or not a sale was made. I confidently expected that the magic number of five closes per call, which both Edwards and Schoonmaker recommended, would turn out to be correct.

Unexpected Results

Our first study took place in a large office-equipment corporation. One way to establish a link between closing and success, we reasoned, would be to travel in the field with sellers and watch how many times they used a closing technique during the call. If the writers on closing were correct, we should expect to find that calls with a lot of closes would be more successful than those where the sellers didn't close so often. We went out and watched a total of 190 calls. From these we took the 30 where the sellers had closed most often and compared their success with the 30 calls where the sellers had closed the least.

As shown in Figure 2.1, the results were not what we'd expected. Only 11 of the high-close calls resulted in a sale, while 21 of the low-

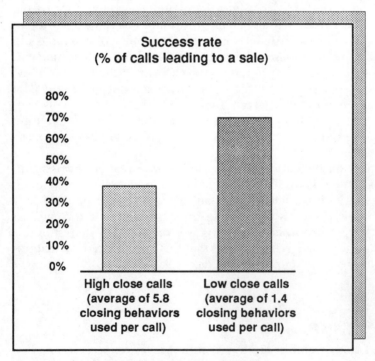

Figure 2.1. Success of high-close versus low-close calls.

close calls did so. This finding wasn't exactly good news for the often-quoted "ideal" figure of five closes per call. But I wasn't discouraged: one small study certainly couldn't shake my faith in closing. Perhaps, I reasoned, there was something wrong with our methodology. Further examination of our results *did* reveal some potential weaknesses. For example, it's possible — just by chance — that the low-close calls were on customers who were prepared to buy anyway, so the seller didn't need to close; similarly, the high-close calls might have been on more resistant customers. Another problem was that our sample, although statistically significant, was small. We had no way to control for intervening variables.

Clearly, just on the basis of this study, we couldn't conclude that closing techniques were ineffective. In a letter to my client explaining our findings, I wrote, "We have not yet succeeded in demonstrating the link between closing and success." But, looking back, we couldn't call this study a resounding victory for the "close early, close hard, and close often" school of selling.

Uneasy Feelings

Research isn't only numbers. By watching closing in 190 calls, I'd begun to get some uneasy feelings that I couldn't quantify. If I'm honest with myself — though I'd not have confessed it at the time — my first misgivings about closing could be traced back to this study. For example, I noticed a distinct antagonism from some customers, especially professional buyers, when any closing technique was used beyond simply asking for the order. In one of the calls, the seller and I were thrown out by an angry customer after an interchange like this:

SELLER: So, Mr. Robinson, you see that our product is clearly best for you — if you'll just sign here. *(Assumptive Close)*

BUYER: Just a moment — I don't see... I haven't decided.

SELLER: But, Mr. Robinson, I've shown you how we can improve the efficiency of your office and save you trouble and also money — so if you could decide when you'd like delivery.... *(Assumptive Close)*

BUYER: I'll do no such thing. I'm not making a decision this week.

SELLER: But as I've explained, this model is in great demand. I can let you have one now, but if you wait till next week, there could be a several-month delay. *(Standing-room-only Close)*

BUYER: That's a risk I'll have to take.

SELLER: Would you prefer a month's trial installation, or would it be better for your budget to buy outright? *(Alternative Close)*

BUYER: I'm going to throw you out of my office. Tell me, would you and your friend in the corner prefer to go of your own accord, or would you like me to call security?

As the seller so ruefully remarked to me after the call, it doesn't seem fair when the buyer uses an Alternative Close to throw you out. We met several episodes like this one and they were enough to sow those first seeds of doubt about closing, particularly in the larger sale.

Attitude Problems

At about this time I had an opportunity to look at closing from a completely different angle. The marketing director of a major chemical company approached us with a problem.

"I'm worried," he said, "about some of my salespeople. They've got a wishy-washy attitude toward closing sales. They're not aggressive enough. I know that they *can* close — they've had training — it's just that some of them have an attitude problem. Can you help?"

It was too good an opportunity to miss. My colleagues and I agreed to devise a closing-attitude scale to compare the salespeople's attitudes with their sales records, hoping ultimately to devise an attitude test that could be used to screen new applicants. Those who scored high on our closing-attitude test should have a greater sales potential. The marketing director and I expected, of course, to find that sellers who had a favorable attitude toward closing should be making more sales.

In order to find the attitude of the 38 members of the sales force, my colleagues and I measured their level of agreement (or disagreement) with 15 key statements about closing. The method we used is what's commonly called a Lickert Scale. If you're the kind of person who likes to test yourself, you'll find that I've included the scale as Appendix B to this book, together with instructions for how to score your own attitude toward closing. You'll probably get a truer picture of how you feel about closing at present if you score the scale now, before you've had a chance to be influenced by the rest of this chapter.

When we used this test in the chemical company, we found that 21 out of 38 sellers had a score above 50, which we had taken to be the minimum score for us to classify their attitude as "favorable." We then compared the sales results to find out whether the group that had a favorable attitude toward closing was, in fact, making more sales. We were taken aback by the results, which are shown in Figure 2.2. As you can see, those sellers with a favorable attitude toward closing were *below* target, not above it. Our hopes for a closing selection test were dashed. What's worse, the marketing director didn't believe the results and threatened to fire me unless I could come up with something more convincing.

As you might imagine, I tried hard to explain away our findings. It was possible, I argued, that those people whose results were poor were made more anxious by being given the test. As a result, they may have

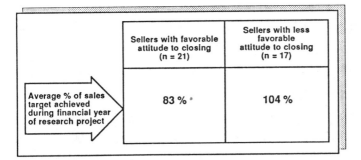

	Sellers with favorable attitude to closing (n = 21)	Sellers with less favorable attitude to closing (n = 17)
Average % of sales target achieved during financial year of research project	83 % *	104 %

Figure 2.2. Attitude to closing and sales results.

cheated and filled in the scale the way they thought management wanted — thus giving those with bad results a falsely positive attitude toward closing. But this sounded unconvincing, even to me. I was beginning to have doubts about the effectiveness of closing.

While we were carrying out this study, a number of research teams all over the world were investigating the links between attitude and behavior. Their results, particularly those of Martin Fishbein,[1] were indicating that you can't use attitude scales to predict behavior accurately. Fishbein was showing, for example, that just because you get a high score on the closing-attitude scale, it doesn't mean that in actual sales calls you'll close more often than those who have a less favorable attitude. Our own research in other areas was confirming that the links between attitude and behavior were much weaker than we'd imagined. Consequently, we were moving more and more toward methods for directly observing sales behavior. We were glad to leave attitude and questionnaire studies behind us. The best test of how people actually perform is to watch them in action. Our development of new behavior-analysis methods would, we hoped, allow us to do this and would provide us with much more solid evidence about the effectiveness of closing.

But even though we found some respectable reasons to dismiss our chemical company study, I was still worried. The little data we had gathered was showing some very puzzling things about closing effectiveness. We needed more studies.

The Effect of Training

An ideal opportunity for further research on closing came when a high-technology company asked us to evaluate some intensive training in

[1]Fishbein, M.; Ajzen I., *Attitudinal Variables and Behavior: Three Empirical Studies and a Theoretical Reanalysis,* 1970, Washington University, Seattle.

closing that it was designing. The company wanted us to answer two questions:

- Did sellers close more often after the training than before it?
- Was there a relationship between increased closing and sales success?

We were delighted to be presented with another opportunity to test the contribution of closing to sales success. We went out on 86 calls with a group of 47 sellers before the training took place. We wanted to find their existing levels of closing.

After the training, we went out with the sellers again, this time to find out whether their use of closing had increased and what effect this had had on the results of their calls. Once again, closing turned out to be negatively related to success. After the training, the sellers used more closing techniques—so in one sense the training was effective. However, because fewer of the calls succeeded, the overall effect of the training was a *decrease* in sales (Figure 2.3).

By now we were much less surprised. Finding an association between

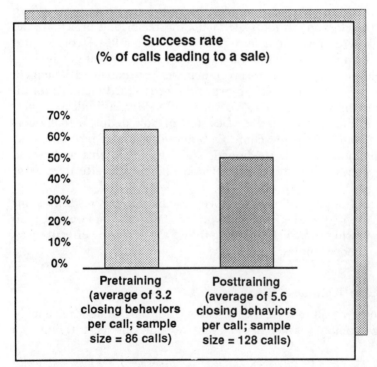

Figure 2.3. Effect of training in closing on success.

closing and lost sales was getting to be a habit with us. The trainers we were working with, on the other hand, certainly didn't expect results like these. They were taken aback and advanced several ingenious explanations for the fall in results. We were forced to take very seriously one of the possibilities they put forward. They argued that, by definition, any new skill feels awkward and uncomfortable. Before the training, the sellers were behaving in their own natural way; after it, they were trying to use new techniques and, inevitably, were not coming across so naturally to their customers. This, the trainers argued, could cause a temporary drop in sales results.

We found this possibility plausible enough to concede that we still didn't have conclusive evidence on the effectiveness of closing. But at least we could test out the idea that the fall in sales resulted from a temporary unnaturalness. What if we went out with the sellers again after 6 months? By that time the new closing skills would have become part of their natural selling style. We could test whether they were still using the closing techniques and, if so, what impact this was now having on the success of their calls. Everything was arranged for what I hoped would be the first conclusive study of closing effectiveness.

Then, a month before the research was due to begin, the company announced a massive reorganization of its sales force. With all the changes, there was no point in going ahead. Another great research study bit the dust and, once again, we found ourselves out in the market looking around for a new company that would give us facilities for studying closing.

A Glimmer of Light

It was while I was searching for a client to sponsor new studies of closing that I came across a claim by one of the big training companies that its program in closing increased sales results by more than 30 percent. In the study we'd just completed, we'd found that training in closing caused a *fall* in results. How was it that this company was achieving success? Could it be using closing techniques that were more effective than the ones we'd been investigating? I managed to get hold of its program and was surprised to find that it didn't contain anything new or different. In fact, it used a considerably less sophisticated approach than the one we'd been evaluating.

So I made contact with the company and challenged it to show me the evidence supporting its claim that training in closing could bring a 30 percent increase in sales. As it happened, the company's "research" consisted of letters from satisfied clients, one of whom had said that after the training there had been a 30 percent increase in results. There was no hard data. But there *was* an important clue. The satisfied clients were all organizations whose size of sale was very small. The 30 percent claimant, for example, was a company selling magazine subscriptions door to door. Then it struck me. All of Huthwaite's studies of closing had been in larger sales. Could it be possible that closing techniques worked when the sale was small, but failed to work as the size of the sale increased?

The more I thought about this idea, the more I liked it. There were very good theoretical reasons for believing that this might be true. Closing is a method of putting pressure on the customer. And psychologists now understand quite a lot about the impact of pressure on making decisions. Put very simply, the psychological effect of pressure seems to be this. If I'm asking you to make a very small decision, then—if I pressure you—it's easier for you to say yes than to have an argument. Consequently, with a small decision, the effect of pressure is positive. But this isn't so with large decisions. The bigger the decision, the more negatively people generally react to pressure.

I make this sound like some great new discovery, but of course it isn't. Since the dawn of history, would-be seducers have known that the effect of pressure is negatively related to the size of the decision. The hopeful young man who uses an Alternative Close such as "Would you prefer that we sit here, or shall we sit over there?" will usually succeed because he's asking for a small decision. However, the classic Alternative Close of "My place or yours?" has a far lower hit rate because the decision it asks for is much larger.

If my theory was correct, then the larger the decision, the less effective the closing techniques were likely to be. But how could we test this? Was there a way to set up an experiment to test the effectiveness of closing as the size of the decision grew larger? I didn't want to set up artificial laboratory experiments, yet I didn't know how to validate the idea in any other way. Then one day we were presented with the perfect opportunity on a plate.

The Photo-Store Study

A leading chain of photographic stores had just decided to train its salespeople in closing techniques. This had been a controversial decision for the chain, and not all of its senior management liked the idea. One of the managers had attended a seminar where I'd spoken rather skeptically about closing. He was from the antitraining faction—and he secretly brought us in to test whether the new training was going to be effective.

It's never ideal when clients ask you to do research designed to prove that their preconceptions are right. Normally this is the kind of assignment we avoid. But everything else about this research opportunity was so perfect that I just couldn't turn it down. The really attractive element was the store's policy of rotating its salespeople. One day a seller would work at a counter that sold cheap goods, such as films, tapes, and accessories. The next day the same person would move to one of the counters where more expensive goods were sold, such as high-priced cameras, hi-fi equipment, and videos. We had the perfect way to control for the impact of decision size on closing success. When the store trained its people, we could observe the impact of the training one day when they were selling cheap goods and then, with the same people and the same training, observe them the next day when they were selling goods on the expensive counters. It was ideal.

Closing and Decision Size

Using the methods taken from our earlier studies, we watched the salespeople at work before the training took place. We measured three things:

1. *Transaction time.* How long did each sale or attempted sale take?

2. *Number of closes.* How often did the seller use a closing behavior during the transaction?

3. *Percentage sale.* What percentage of the transactions resulted in a purchase?

First, let's look at the results collected when people were selling low-value items (Figure 2.4). Before training in closing, the average transaction time was just over 2 minutes, the seller used an average of 1.3 closes, and 72 percent of the transactions resulted in a sale. What was the effect of the closing training? As you can see, after training the transaction time was shortened, the number of closes increased, and so did the success rate. As a busy store owner, I would be delighted with a result like this. The shortened transaction time means that I can serve more customers or use fewer staff. What's more, although the increase in sales from 72 to 76 percent isn't big enough to be statistically significant, it *is* in the right direction. Not only is the sale faster, but it also looks to be more successful.

We, too, were impressed with these results, if only because it was the first time in our research that we'd found anything positive about closing techniques. But the real test was yet to come. Would the training in closing be equally successful with higher-value goods?

We observed the same salespeople after the same training. The only

	Average transaction time	Number of closes per transaction	% transactions resulting in a sale
Before training in closing (83 transactions observed)	2 min 11 sec	1.3	72%
After training in closing (95 transactions observed)	1 min 47 sec	1.9	76%

Figure 2.4. Closing and price: low-value goods.

difference was that they were now selling more expensive items. We found that the transaction time after the training was shorter and that the number of closing behaviors predictably increased (Figure 2.5). But what about the success rate? Before the training, 42 percent of the interactions we observed had resulted in an order. This was much lower than the success rate with cheaper goods, but it was hardly surprising. People don't usually come into a store to look at a roll of film and say,

	Average transaction time	Number of closes per transaction	% transactions resulting in a sale
Before training in closing (91 transactions observed)	12 min 35 sec	2.7	42%
After training in closing (91 transactions observed)	8 min 40 sec	4.5	33%

Figure 2.5. Closing and price: high-value goods.

"I'll go away and think about it," although this often happens with more expensive purchases. However, the figure that interested us was the success rate after training. We found that the program in closing, which had increased the success with cheap goods, had *reduced* the success with more expensive goods from 42 percent down to 33 percent.

Two Conclusions

How should we interpret these results? The first finding is that, with both high- and low-value goods, the average transaction time is reduced as the number of closes is increased. So we can draw the conclusion:

By forcing the customer into a decision, closing techniques speed the sales transaction.

This would be an important finding—and a big plus for the use of closing techniques—if your business were a low-value retail operation or involved door-to-door selling of low-value products. If there's a queue of customers waiting for your attention, or an infinitely long street with doors on both sides just waiting to be knocked on, then the shorter the sale, the more customers you'll be able to serve.

But this is not usually the problem in larger sales. You normally want *more* time with each customer, not less. In most major-account sales forces, the most common complaint is that you can't get *enough* time with the right people. I don't think I've ever heard anyone in larger sales say, "How can I cut down on the time I'm spending with key decision makers?" However, a number of companies have called Huthwaite in to advise them on ways to *increase* sales time with customers. My point's a simple one: In small sales it's generally desirable to keep the transaction time short; in larger sales—for a whole variety of reasons—a shorter transaction time has few advantages and many penalties.

The second conclusion we can draw from our study is about the relationship of closing to price:

Closing techniques may increase the chances of making a sale with low-priced products. With expensive products or services, they reduce the chances of making a sale.

As we've seen, this conclusion comes not only from our research but also from the general psychological rule that pressure is more likely to be effective with small decisions than with larger ones. The average price of the high-value goods in our study was just $109. That's peanuts compared with the average decision size in most sales organizations I work with, or for most readers of this book. But if closing techniques become ineffective in a $109 sale, then they are likely to be even more ineffective as the size of the decision climbs into the tens or hundreds of thousands. You might argue, of course, that spending $109 of your own money may feel just as big a decision as spending $10,000 from a company budget. And you might be right—nobody really understands the complex psychology of perceived decision size. But the general rule remains. Closing techniques, like all forms of pressure, become less effective as decision size increases.

Closing and Client Sophistication

It was clear from our studies that closing is less effective as the size of the decision increases. But is this just because of price factors? I wondered whether there might be some other reasons. On the whole, large purchasing decisions are made by more sophisticated customers—such as professional purchasing agents or senior executives. These people see dozens of sellers each week and may even have been through sales training themselves. Could it be that a closing technique that might work on a less experienced buyer would be ineffective or even have a negative effect on customers who were more sophisticated?

My first indication that this might be true came when I was working with the central purchasing department of British Petroleum. I'd been observing their buyers at work, doing research from the other side of the table. One of the BP senior buyers was particularly ill-disposed toward the use of closing techniques. "It's not closing itself that I object to," he told me, "it's the arrogant assumption that I'm stupid enough to be manipulated into buying through the use of tricks. Whenever a standard closing technique is used on me, it reduces the respect between us—it destroys the professional business relationship. But I've got my own way of dealing with it, as you'll see."

The following day I was watching an attempted sale and saw the buyer's method in action. The seller was in the vending machine business and supplied plastic cups. At one point in the call he used an Assumptive Close, saying "Mr. P., you've agreed that our cups are cheaper than your present supplier, so shall we make our first delivery of, say, 20,000 cups next month?" The buyer said nothing. He opened a drawer in his desk and slowly took out a box of 3 × 5 index cards. He shuffled through the box and selected one with ASSUMPTIVE CLOSE typed on it, placing it face up on his desk. "That's your first chance," he said. "I give people two. If you use just one more closing technique on me, then it's no sale. Just so you know what I'm watching for, look through these cards." And he handed the cards across his desk to the seller. On each card a well-known closing technique was typed. The seller went pale—but didn't try closing again.

Was this buyer an exception? Some monster with a perverted hatred of closing? I don't think so. Most professional buyers have an unfavorable view of closing techniques. I once trained professional buyers from three large organizations in a program that developed negotiating skills. I circulated a questionnaire among 54 of these buyers that included the question:

If you detect that a seller is using closing techniques while selling to you, what effect, if any, does this have on your likelihood of buying?

Their answers were:

More likely to buy	2
Indifferent	18
Less likely to buy	34

Nobody knows better than I do that this type of questionnaire data isn't a very reliable guide to actual behavior. But despite all the limitations of this kind of evidence, closing techniques certainly don't seem to be favorites with professional buyers. I've seen a number of books and training programs which claim that sophisticated buyers react very positively to the use of closing techniques because it's a sign that they're dealing with a professional. That's dangerous nonsense. There's not one scrap of evidence to back that sort of assertion. The few existing research studies all suggest that the more sophisticated buyers react negatively to the use of closing.

Closing and Post-Sale Satisfaction

In Chapter 1, I pointed out that one of the characteristic differences between small and large sales is that larger sales usually involve some form of ongoing relationship with the customer. Your job doesn't just end with the order. So it's an important question to ask what effect closing has on the post-sale relationship. Unfortunately we've never had an opportunity to study this in larger sales. However, we did help one retail organization carry out a consumer goods study that proved to have some disturbing implications for sales of *any* size.

The training manager of a retail chain had attended a seminar run by

Huthwaite on behavior measurement, and he was keen to try his hand at some research. He asked me for help in choosing a suitable project. "How about a study on closing?" I suggested. Some of the salespeople in his organization had been trained in closing techniques, so he decided to investigate whether customer satisfaction after the purchase was related to the seller's training in closing.

Between 3 and 5 days after the purchase, he and his team followed up 145 customers and asked them to rate, on a 10-point scale:

- Their satisfaction with the goods they had purchased

- The probability, if they were to make similar purchases in the future, that they would buy from the same store

As shown in Figure 2.6, the sellers who had been trained in closing had lower satisfaction ratings on both questions. What does this mean? The most likely interpretation is that, in using closing techniques, the sellers put pressure on customers to make a decision. Most people are less satisfied with decisions that they feel they've been pressured to make than with those which they believe they've made entirely of their own free will. This suggests that there's even more reason to be cautious about the use of closing techniques in larger sales, where the customer's post-sale satisfaction may be an important factor in future selling success.

I could, of course, criticize some elements of this study. For example, it doesn't have any behavioral data collected during the actual sales

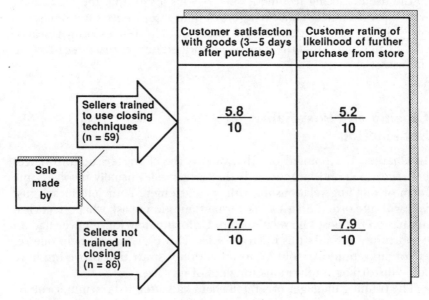

Figure 2.6. Closing and customer satisfaction.

themselves. And there's another possible weakness—the store had trained more of its younger people than its most experienced sellers. So perhaps this study is saying that customers are less satisfied with purchases from more junior salespeople. But despite any criticisms of its methodology, this study is one of the very few that has ever tried to collect data on the relationship between sales training and post-sale satisfaction. Until more detailed studies comes along, I advise you to heed its warning.

Why Is the Rest of the Army out of Step?

For several years after I'd collected all this data about the effectiveness of closing, I was very reluctant to share it with people. As I showed early in this chapter, closing was not only seen by the majority of writers to be the most important part of the sale, it was also almost a religion with many salespeople. On the few occasions when I'd mentioned these findings in public, I'd had a bad reception. I was once pulled off the stage by an angry sales trainer in Los Angeles who didn't like the research I've presented here. History is full of stories about researchers whose ideas aren't recognized at first, but it wasn't the rejection that worried me. My concern was that it didn't seem possible that I was right and so many others were wrong. Experienced salespeople, their managers, their trainers, and the experts who write books on how to sell aren't fools. How could they be devoting so much time and energy to a set of techniques that not only don't work but, in larger sales, are actively counterproductive? What's so compelling about closing?

What Makes a Compulsive Closer?

The answer came to me during a seminar I was running with the California management consultant Roger Harrison. In one session that Roger was conducting, the topic was ineffective behavior patterns and their causes. He explained to the class that sometimes people continue to do things that don't bring results, all the while believing strongly that what they are doing is effective. "Hmm, like salespeople who believe in closing," I thought. Roger went on to suggest that there are only two reasons why people would continue to behave in an unsuccessful way. Either they are crazy or *there's something in their environment that's rewarding and encouraging the use of the ineffective behavior.*

The more I thought about this, the more it gave me the explanation I'd been looking for. I remembered the time when I, too, had been so enthusiastic about closing. How did I get "hooked" into becoming a hard closer? It all went back to the time I nervously tried my first Alternative Close: "Would you prefer the project to begin in September or in November?" In replying "Let's start in September," my client *rewarded* my use of a close by giving me the business. I said the words—I got the order.

When I stopped to think about it, closing behaviors were the only ones, out of the 116 we studied in our research, that were directly rewarded or reinforced by orders. Like so many other salespeople, because my close was rewarded with an order, I'd somehow assumed that using the close had *caused* the order. Of course, from what I now know, it was the way I'd developed my client's needs that had brought me the business. It had nothing to do with my close. The project would have gone ahead with or without my new closing technique.

At last I understood why closing received so much attention in selling. It was the most immediately rewarded of all sales behaviors. Ask the customer a good question that develops needs and you don't instantly get rewarded with an order. But use some magic closing catch phrase at the moment of decision and—some of the time—you'll get a rewarding "Yes, I'll buy." (Incidentally, any reader who understands the theory of reinforcement will also recognize that "some of the time" rewards are even more powerful than "all of the time" rewards in causing a behavior to continue.)

As a result of this insight, I became more comfortable about our research and its implications. It was indeed possible that our research was right and most of the rest of the world was out of step. Since our studies, of course, many other people have come to the same conclusion that closing techniques are ineffective or even damaging in larger sales. I'm delighted nowadays, when I talk to people about closing, to find that I no longer get the antagonism that our work once aroused. I've been seen by many people as a sworn enemy of all closing techniques. If J. Douglas Edwards is the father of closing, I've sometimes been described as its assassin. But that's not quite fair. In low-value sales, given unsophisticated customers and no need to develop a continuing customer relationship, closing techniques can work very effectively—and I've no criticism of their use. But I'm assuming that, as a reader of this book, your business comes from the larger sale, that you deal with professional buyers, and that you form lasting relationships with your customers. If so, then closing techniques will make you *less* effective and will reduce your chances of getting the business.

But You *Must* Close

It may sound as though I'm saying that you shouldn't try to close the sale—that because closing techniques are ineffective, you should somehow wait for the sale to close itself—but clearly this doesn't work either.

Many sales managers have groaned inwardly as they've listened to their less experienced people reach the Obtaining Commitment stage of the call and then fail to close. They've heard something like this:

NEW SELLER: So, is there anything else I can tell you about this product?

CUSTOMER: No thanks. I think you've answered all my questions.

NEW SELLER: Good. Good. You're sure there's nothing else I haven't covered?

CUSTOMER: Not that I can think of.

NEW SELLER: OK *(horrid pause)* uh...perhaps I didn't mention that it's got dual voltage.

CUSTOMER: Yes. Well I'm overdue for another meeting and...

NEW SELLER: *(with some desperation)* It's also got an instruction manual in Spanish...if you need Spanish.

CUSTOMER: Look, Mr. Newman, I've got to go.

NEW SELLER: Um. Are you *sure* I've answered all your questions?

What's wrong here? An inexperienced salesperson is afraid to bring the call to a conclusion and, as a result, the customer is getting impatient.

This certainly happens in real life—and it's often noticeable in the selling of professional services. We've worked with First National Bank of Chicago, using Huthwaite's models to train calling officers. David Zehren of First Chicago, while agreeing with us that closing techniques are generally overused in major industrial sales, points out that in banking there's often the opposite problem. "We haven't had a problem with excessive use of closing techniques," he explains. "If anything, we feel it necessary to lean in the other direction. Customers expect it. They get irritated by calls that don't have a clear understanding of what comes next."

David Zehren isn't the only one to voice this concern. We've worked with several of the big eight accounting firms, and their training staffs share the same perception. If the overuse of closing is a problem in many industrial and capital goods sales, then its total absence may be an equally severe problem in some service industries. While most of our clients fully accept that the most crucial part of the sales call is developing needs, those in the professional services area justifiably want their people to take a stronger role in obtaining commitment from customers.

Sales training, over the years, has clearly put much too great an emphasis on closing. But it would be equally unfortunate if we let the pendulum swing so far the other way that we began to teach people never to close at all.

There's hard data to support the conclusion that an absence of closing can be a real danger. We conducted some research with Bob Boyles

of American Airlines to find out whether the complete absence of closing was even less effective than closing too often. Boyles and his team
had been experimenting with some of our behavior-analysis techniques
in American Airlines to monitor the skills of their sales agents.

The success rate in calls with no closing whatsoever was only 22 percent, compared with a 61 percent success rate in one-close calls (Figure
2.7). Notice, however, that the least successful calls were those with
more than two closing behaviors, where the success rate was below 20
percent. So it seems that, despite all the disadvantages of closing techniques, calls with no closing whatsoever are unlikely to be effective.

Where Do We Go from Here?

The American Airlines investigation involved relatively small sales. Although I'm not sure whether we'd have found the same results in a
comparable study of major sales, this research does raise an important
issue. The seller *must* obtain some kind of commitment from the customer for the call to be a success. But how can you get a commitment
from your customer without risking the penalties that come from using
closing techniques?

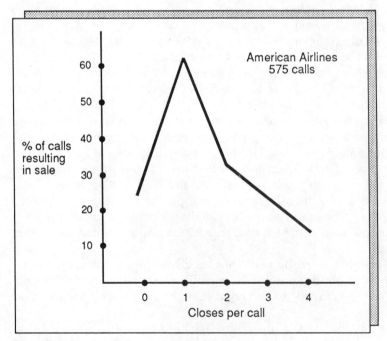

Figure 2.7. Number of closes versus success rate.

Everything I've written so far in this chapter is about how *not* to obtain commitment. I've said that traditional closing techniques are ineffective or have a negative effect when:

- The sale is large, involving high-value goods.
- The customer is sophisticated: for example, a professional buyer.
- There is a continuing post-sale relationship with the customer.

All that I've said suggests that closing techniques are not the best way to obtain commitment from the customer in a major sale. But what *should* you do? As we've seen, doing nothing isn't effective either. The sale doesn't close itself.

Obtaining the *Right* Commitment

The first step in successful closing is to set the right objectives. The starting point for obtaining a commitment is to know what level of commitment from the customer will be needed to make the call a success. If this book was about simpler sales, then there wouldn't be much need to explain what *success* means or to worry about its detailed definition. In a simple sale, a successful commitment is an order—and if you don't take an order, you've failed.

So, closing in a simple sale can have one of two outcomes—an *Order,* where you take the business, or a *No-sale,* where the customer turns you down. But as the sale becomes larger, it's not so straightforward. In major sales, relatively few calls result in an Order or a No-sale. Earlier I mentioned the case of a friend in the aircraft industry who went for 3 whole years without taking an order. At the same time, he didn't have any outright refusals that could be called No-sales. All his calls were somewhere in between. They made slow but modest progress toward his ultimate goal—an order in several years' time.

In most major-account sales forces, fewer than 10 percent of calls result in an Order or No-sale. In these larger sales it becomes more difficult to judge whether a call has been closed successfully. For example, suppose you're selling me a computer software package to help me with my inventory control. At the end of the call, I say to you, "Look, I'm convinced that your inventory system is what we need. But I can't make such an important decision alone, so I'd like to fix for you to come back next week and talk to our production controller." It's clear that the call has achieved something, yet it hasn't resulted in either an Order or a No-sale. It's somewhere in between. However, because it's brought about another meeting, perhaps we could say that the call has been successfully closed.

But can we say this about *every* call that results in an agreement to a further meeting? Suppose, after you've explained the benefits of your inventory system, I say, "I'm not sure. Perhaps we could talk about it again some other time. Why don't you call me in a few months to fix another meeting." It's quite possible that I'm agreeing to a future meeting just to get rid of you. When you call next month you won't be able to get through to me and the meeting may never happen. Just getting an agreement to a future meeting isn't an adequate measure of whether you've closed successfully.

Defining Closing Success in Larger Sales

So what's the test of closing success? What's the result, or outcome, that allows us to say that one call has been successful while another has failed? In our early research at Huthwaite we took the coward's way out. We said that a call was successful if it met its objectives. But I soon discovered that the amazing human capacity to rationalize away unwanted events would make this definition unworkable.

I'd been traveling with a sales rep in New York City. We made a disastrous call on a customer who became so irritated with the sales rep that we were asked to leave. Afterward, as we stood on the sidewalk recovering from the experience, I was filling in call details on my research form. In response to the question "Did the call meet its objectives?" I wrote, "No." This upset the sales rep mightily.

"But I *did* meet my objectives," he protested. "I decided, part way through the call, that we didn't want to do business with this guy because he sounded like a poor credit risk. So, rather than insult him by telling him this directly, I engineered things so he threw us out. In this way I was able to terminate the call without the embarrassment of explaining that I couldn't do business with him because his credit was poor."

Over and over again, in our early research, we had salespeople respond in this way, telling us that whatever happened in the call had been exactly what they had planned. Call objectives can too easily be rationalized afterward to fit the events. Obviously we needed a better criterion of closing success than the simple question "Did the call meet its objectives?"

Our next attempt was a little better. We asked the seller to give us objectives *in advance*. We then assessed whether the call had succeeded in meeting the objectives we'd been given. In this way we were able to prevent sellers from rationalizing away their failed calls. But it wasn't a perfect system. I remember one person telling me in advance that the objective of her call was "detailed exploration of the customer's organization structure." At the start of the call, the customer unexpectedly revealed that, as a result of an evaluation his firm had carried out, he had decided to place a major order with the seller. She and I walked away, an hour later, with all the paperwork completed for $35,000 of business, but she didn't find out a single thing about organization structure. Yet one could hardly say that the call was ineffectively closed just because this initial objective hadn't been met.

We still needed a better way to measure closing success.

The method we finally chose involved dividing the possible outcomes of the call into four areas (Figure 2.8):

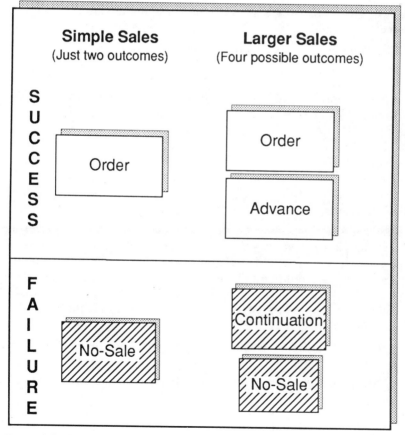

Figure 2.8. Call outcomes and sales success.

■ Orders

Where the customer makes a firm commitment to buy. "We're 99.9 percent likely to buy" would *not* be an order, as generations of sales managers have wearily pointed out to their new and inexperienced people. To be an order, the customer must show an unmistakable intention to purchase, usually by signing some kind of paperwork. Needless to say, calls that result in orders are less common in larger sales than most sellers would like. So there are relatively few occasions when you can close for the order.

■ Advances

Where an event takes place, either in the call or after it, that moves the sale forward toward a decision. Typical Advances might include:

- A customer's agreement to attend an off-site demonstration
- A clearance that will get you in front of a higher level of decision maker
- An agreement to run a trial or test of your product
- Access to parts of the account that were previously inaccessible to you

All of these represent an agreement with the customer that moves the sale forward toward the ultimate decision. Advances take many forms, but invariably they involve an *action* that moves the sale forward. In larger sales the most common objective of closing would normally be to obtain an Advance. Successful closing in the major sale starts by knowing what Advance you can realistically obtain from the call.

■ Continuations

Where the sale will continue but where no specific action has been agreed upon by the customer to move it forward. These calls don't result in an agreed action, yet neither do they involve a "No" from the customer. Typical examples would be calls that end with a customer saying:

- "Thank you for coming. Why don't you visit us again the next time you're in the area."
- "Fantastic presentation, we're very impressed. Let's meet again some time."
- "We liked what we saw and we'll be in touch if we need to take things further."

In none of these cases has the buyer agreed to a specific action, so there's no concrete sign that the sale has progressed. In our studies, we classified calls that closed with Continuations as unsuccessful. This may strike you as a little unfair. After all, it seems harsh to say that a call has been closed unsuccessfully if the customer says positive things, such as "We're impressed" or "That was a great presentation." However, having worked closely with buyers over the years, I can no longer accept positive strokes and compliments as reliable signs of call success. Too often I've seen customers make these positive noises at the end of a call as a polite way to get rid of an unwanted seller. In our studies we wanted closing success to be measured by *actions,* not by nice noises. That's why we classified Advances as successful and Continuations as unsuccessful. Whether a call has been successfully closed should be judged by customers' actions, not by their words.

■ No-sales

Our final category is *where the customer actively refuses a commitment.* At an extreme, the No-sale customer makes it clear that there's no possibility of any business. In a lesser way, it can be a No-sale if the customer won't agree to a future meeting, say, or denies your request to see a more senior person in the account. The test of a No-sale is that the customer *actively* denies you your principal call objective. There's not much dispute that a call resulting in No-sale should be classified as unsuccessful.

Why am I making such a fuss about the different outcomes of a sales call? "Surely," a critic might say, "only researchers are interested in defining call outcomes. There's nothing useful here for helping people close more sales." On the contrary. Our studies of top salespeople consistently showed that they had a clear understanding of these different outcomes and that they used this understanding to help them close calls more effectively by turning Continuations into Advances. What's more, by understanding what kind of Advance would be required to make a call successful, top people set the kind of realistic closing objectives that moved major sales forward.

Let me illustrate this by contrasting the performance of two salespeople, each selling industrial pumping equipment. First, let's look at John C. He's relatively inexperienced, having spent only a year in major sales. In this extract from an interview with him, judge for yourself whether he's clear about the difference between an Advance and a Continuation and whether he understands how this difference relates to success in closing the call:

> INTERVIEWER: What were your objectives for this call?
> JOHN C.: Oh,...to make a good impression on the customer.
> INTERVIEWER: "Good impression"?

JOHN C.: Well, yes, making the customer feel positive about us.

INTERVIEWER: And any other objective?

JOHN C.: To collect data.

INTERVIEWER: Data? What kind of data?

JOHN C.: Oh, useful facts. Stuff about the account. Just general information.

INTERVIEWER: And were you trying to get a specific *action* from the customer?

JOHN C.: No. Like I say, it was mostly building a relationship and finding facts.

INTERVIEWER: In your judgment, how successful was the call?

JOHN C.: Quite successful, I think.

INTERVIEWER: Why do you say that?

JOHN C.: Well, for example, the customer said he was impressed by my presentation.

INTERVIEWER: Did the customer agree to any *actions* as a result of the call?

JOHN C.: Uh,...no. But I think he liked my presentation.

INTERVIEWER: So what will happen next with this customer?

JOHN C.: We'll meet again in a couple of months and then we'll take things further.

INTERVIEWER: But, looking back on the call you just made, the customer didn't agree to an action that moved the sale forward?

JOHN C.: No. But I'm sure the call contributed to building a good relationship with the account. That's why I think it was a successful call.

John C.'s reaction is typical of inexperienced sellers. He thinks he's closed the call successfully because he received some positive strokes from the customer. But, turning to our definitions of call outcomes, his call has resulted in a *Continuation*. There's been no specific action agreed upon by the customer that progresses the sale. Like many new salespeople, John's call objectives—collect data and build a relationship—don't directly contribute to getting an Advance. After I traveled with John, his manager told me, "You know what John's problem is? He's a weak closer. I wish someone would teach him a few good closing techniques." I'd prefer to say John's problem was that he didn't know what Advance he was seeking from the call. Consequently, he didn't have anything to close for. His problem was one of call objectives, and there's nothing that closing techniques could do to help his success until he was clearer about the difference between a Continuation and an Advance.

In contrast, let's hear Fred F., one of the company's top salespeople, talking about his approach to a typical call:

INTERVIEWER: What were your call objectives?

FRED F.: I wanted to get some *movement* because I knew we'd meet competitive pressure and I didn't want to let the grass grow under my feet.

INTERVIEWER: Movement?

FRED F.: Yes. You see, I feel that if a call's worth making, it's got to *do* something—to push the sale forward in some way. Otherwise, you're wasting both your time and the customer's.

INTERVIEWER: Could you give me an example of a call objective that shows this "movement"?

FRED F.: Sure. In this case what I wanted was to get their chief engineer to come to our factory for a feasibility discussion with our technical people. Now that takes the sale a step forward—and it would also mean that while he was talking with us he wouldn't be spending time with the competition.

INTERVIEWER: And was the call successful?

FRED F.: Yes and no. I didn't get their chief engineer because of some internal issues. So in that sense I failed. But during the call I saw a chance to go forward in another area. The customer told me that they've just gotten the go-ahead to build a new plant in Jersey. They're setting up a project team to write specifications and choose suppliers. So I asked him if he'd call the team's hydraulics engineer and fix a meeting for me.

INTERVIEWER: And he did?

FRED F.: Yes, we meet on the 23d.

INTERVIEWER: And that moves you forward?

FRED F.: Of course. It puts me in on the ground floor. On the 23d I'll try to get their hydraulics guy to specify us as a supplier both for pumps and specialist pipework.

Notice how Fred F.'s objectives were about getting an *action,* or Advance, and that he judged the call's success in terms of the movement it produced. It's this action-oriented approach that characterized the successful people we studied. They wanted Advances, not Continuations. It was their clarity about what constituted a realistic Advance that allowed them to know what they were closing for in the call. People who consistently aim for Advances rather than Continuations are often described by their managers as "good closers." In fact, their success comes from how they set call objectives rather than from how they close. Fred F. was highly regarded by his management as a strong closer, but in the several calls we made with him we didn't see him use any closing techniques.

I'm often asked by sales managers for advice on how they should coach their people to close more successfully in major sales. The simplest and most effective advice I can offer is this: Teach your people the difference between Continuations and Advances, and help them become dissatisfied with setting call objectives that result only in a Continuation.

Setting Call Objectives

The secret of strong closing in a major-account call is to question your objectives ruthlessly. Don't be content with objectives like "to collect information" or "to build a good relationship." Of course, these are important objectives—after all, *every* call affords opportunities to collect information and to improve relationships. The problem is that objectives of this kind just aren't enough. They lead to Continuations, not to Advances. They may lead you to close for the wrong objective.

In your call planning, always include objectives that result in *specific action* from the customer—objectives like "To get her to come to a demonstration," "To get a meeting with his boss," or "To get an introduction to the Planning Department." In this way you'll be planning like the top salespeople in our study. You'll be looking for Advances, not for Continuations.

Obtaining Commitment: Four Successful Actions

But however well you set your call objectives, you've still got to gain the customer's commitment and acceptance. Huthwaite's studies of success in the major sale show that effective salespeople use rather simple and straightforward ways of obtaining commitment. We found that there are four clear actions that successful people tend to use to help them obtain commitment from their customers:

1. *Giving attention to Investigating and Demonstrating Capability.* Successful salespeople give their primary attention to the Investigating and Demonstrating Capability stages. In particular, they take much more time over the Investigating part of the call (Figure 2.9). Less successful sellers rush through the Investigating stage; as a result, they don't do such an effective job of uncovering, understanding, and developing the needs of their customers.

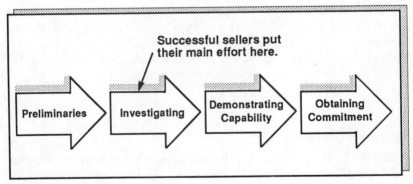

Figure 2.9. Four stages of a sales call.

You won't obtain commitment in a major sale unless the customer clearly perceives a need for what you offer. The most effective people we observed were the ones who did an outstanding job of building needs during the Investigating stage. As a result of the questions they asked, their customers came to realize that they had an urgent need to buy. You don't require closing techniques with a customer who wants to buy. So the first successful strategy for obtaining customer commitment is to concentrate your attention on the Investigating stage of the call. If you can convince buyers that they need what you are offering, then they will often close the sale for you.

2. *Checking that key concerns are covered.* In larger sales, both the product and the customer's needs are likely to be relatively complex. As a result, there may well be areas of confusion or doubt in the customer's mind as the point of commitment nears. Less successful sellers go ahead and close, ignoring the possibility that their customers may still have unanswered questions. This is often how they've been taught to sell. Most sales-training programs actually recommend that you use closing as a means of bringing doubts or unanswered questions to the surface, but this is not what successful salespeople do. We found that sellers who were most effective in obtaining commitment from their customers would invariably take the initiative and ask the buyer whether there were any further points or concerns that needed to be addressed.

From our observations, a doubt or concern that is given in response to a closing technique tends to be antagonistic, as this brief example illustrates:

> SELLER: *(using Assumptive Close)*...so I'll arrange for our technical people to set up a demonstration next week.
> BUYER: *(who has an unresolved concern)* Hey, wait a minute, I'm not sure whether I'm ready for a demonstration.
> SELLER: *(using Alternative Close)* Then would it be better if, instead of setting it up for next week, I set it up for the week after?
> BUYER: *(feeling pressured)* Now, not so fast. You still haven't explained how this leasing arrangement would work. What are you trying to hide?

By using closing techniques, it's true that the seller has brought the customer's concern to the surface. But was it necessary to do so in such an antagonistic way?

A more successful seller would have checked that all key concerns were covered before trying to bring the call to a conclusion. For example:

> SELLER: *(checking that all key concerns are covered)* Well, I think that covers everything, Ms. Brown. But before we go further, could I check whether there are any areas that you feel I should tell you more about?

> BUYER: Yes, you haven't mentioned the terms of the leasing arrangement.
> SELLER: Then let me cover that now. The way it works is...

In this example, the customer's concern has been brought to the surface by the seller's initiative. Instead of being an antagonistic protest from the buyer, it has become a simple query.

3. *Summarizing the Benefits.* In a larger sale the call may have taken several hours and covered a wide range of topics. It's unlikely that the customer has a clear picture of everything that has been discussed. Successful salespeople pull the threads together by summarizing key points of the discussion before moving to the commitment. In smaller sales, the use of a summary may not be necessary, but in a larger sale it will almost always be a helpful way to bring key points into focus just before the decision. So, summarize key points—especially Benefits.

4. *Proposing a commitment.* Many books on selling point out that the simplest of all closing methods is just to ask for the order. Consequently, the phrase "asking for the order" is a common one in sales training. But from our studies, "asking" is *not* what successful sellers do. In all the other stages of the sale, asking behaviors are much more successful than giving behaviors—as we'll see later. But it's here, at the point of commitment, that successful sellers don't ask—they tell. The most natural, and most effective, way to bring a call to a successful conclusion is to suggest an appropriate next step to the customer. For example:

> SELLER: *(checking key concerns)* Is there anything else that we need to cover?
> BUYER: No, I think we've discussed everything.
> SELLER: *(summarizing the benefits)* Yes, we've certainly seen how the new system will speed your order processing and how it will be simpler to use than your present one. We've also discussed the way in which it can help you control costs. In fact, there seem to be some impressive benefits from changing, particularly as a new system would get rid of those reliability problems which have been worrying you.
> BUYER: Yes, when you add it all up, there's a lot of value to us from making the change.
> SELLER: *(proposing a commitment)* Then I might suggest that the most logical next step would be for you and your accountant to come and see one of these systems in operation.

How do you know which commitment to propose? Put simply, there are two characteristics of the commitments proposed by successful salespeople:

1. The commitment *advances* the sale. As a result of the commitment, the sale will move forward in some way.

2. The commitment proposed is the highest *realistic* commitment that the customer is able to give. Successful sellers never push the customer beyond achievable limits.

I've saved the last word on closing the sale for an old friend and colleague of mine, the Swedish consultant Hans Stennek. At a time when my research was controversial and was generally rejected by most people in selling, Hans was very supportive. "I've never been a believer in closing," he told me, "because my objective is not to close the sale but to open a relationship." I couldn't have said it better.

3
Customer Needs in the Major Sale

I suggested in Chapter 2 that success in the Obtaining Commitment stage of the call depends on how well the earlier stages have been handled. Our studies at Huthwaite revealed that the stage with the strongest influence on overall call success is Investigating (Figure 3.1).

In our research we consistently found that the people who were most effective during the Investigating stage were the ones most likely to be top sales performers. And poor investigating skills made sellers seem weak in the later stages of the call. Over and over again we'd find that salespeople who were described by their managers as "weak closers" were, in fact, unskilled in Investigating. I've always derived a sneaky delight when, after a program we've run for salespeople, their managers tell us things like "You really did a great job beefing up Fred's closing" or "Ann's now a much stronger closer, so you must have taught her

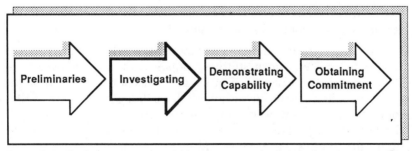

Figure 3.1. The Investigating stage: Asking questions and collecting data about customers, their business, and their needs.

some dynamite techniques." In fact, we've given very little attention to closing. Our main objective in the training has been to improve Investigating skills by teaching people how to develop customer needs using the SPIN questions. And that brings me to the subject of this chapter—customer needs.

As the sale grows in size, customer needs begin to develop in a different way than in small sales. Let me first give you an example of how needs develop in a very small sale. A few months ago I was waiting for a connecting flight in Atlanta. As I wandered through an airport store, a small gadget caught my eye. It was one of those multibladed tools with screwdrivers, a knife, and a device for extracting mysterious objects from unlikely places. It came in a neat little leather pouch and it cost about $15. Within 2 seconds of seeing it I was reaching for my wallet. My need developed all the way from nothing to the point of purchase in a lot less time than it takes you to read this sentence.

In contrast, the first time I bought a computer system there was upwards of a year between initial discussions about our needs and the final decision. It's in the nature of major sales that needs aren't instant. They develop slowly and sometimes painfully. Major sales require special selling skills to help this process of needs development—and these skills represent some of the most crucial differences between success in small sales and in large.

Different Needs in Small Sales and Large

Let's look more closely at my $15 decision and see what it illustrates about needs in the small sale. Clearly the most obvious and dramatic aspect is the faster speed of needs development in smaller sales. But there are other contrasts with larger sales that are worth noting. For example:

- It was exclusively *my* need I was satisfying. I didn't have to consult with others, as I would almost certainly do in a major sale.

- My need had a strong emotional component. I didn't have a rational use for the gadget, and it still lies unopened on the back shelf reserved for why-on-earth-did-I-buy-that acquisitions. If I'd thought more carefully, I probably wouldn't have bought it. Spur-of-the-moment decisions, often irrational ones, are more common in small sales than in large. The emotional component of needs *does* exist in larger sales, but it's more subtle and more subdued.

- If I'd make a bad purchase that didn't really meet my needs, the worst thing that could happen would be the loss of $15. In contrast, a bad purchasing decision in a major sale could cost me my job.

A $15 purchase is, of course, tiny even in terms of small sales. But it illustrates some key differences between needs in small sales and in large. Broadly speaking, we can say that as the sale becomes larger:

- Needs take longer to develop.
- Needs are likely to involve elements, influences, and inputs from several people, not just the wishes of a single individual.
- Needs are more likely to be expressed on a rational basis, and even if the customer's underlying motivation is emotional or irrational, the need will usually require a rational justification.
- A purchasing decision that doesn't adequately meet needs is likely to have more serious consequences for the decision maker.

Are these differences substantial enough to require different questioning skills when you're developing needs in a larger sale? Our research suggests that they are. We found that some of the probing techniques that were very successful in smaller sales failed entirely in larger ones.

In order to understand why questioning skills are different in larger sales, we must first be clear about the stages through which needs develop. Let's begin with a definition of what we mean by *need*. In our research, we defined a need as:

Any statement made by the buyer which expresses a want or concern that can be satisfied by the seller.

Incidentally, some writers have made great play of the distinction between a need and a want. A need, they say, is an objective requirement—you *need* a car because there's no other form of transport that will get you to work. A want, on the other hand, is something that has personal emotional appeal—you *want* a Rolls Royce, but this doesn't mean that you need one. We found this distinction unhelpful, particularly in larger sales. When we refer to the term *need*, we use the word in a broad sense. Our definition includes both the needs and wants that the buyer expresses.

How Needs Develop

A potential buyer who genuinely feels 100 percent satisfied with the way things are doesn't feel any need to change. What's the first sign—in any of us—that we have a need? Our 100 percent satisfaction with the existing situation becomes a 99.9 percent satisfaction. We can no longer genuinely say that we feel absolutely content with the way things are. So the first sign of a need is a slight discontent or dissatisfaction.

A few months ago, for example, I could honestly say that I was completely satisfied with the word processor I'm using to type this book. I had no need, and if you were selling word processors, I'd have been a wasted call. However, while writing this, I've become more aware of a few small imperfections. The automatic spelling check is cumbersome to use. Certain editing functions are a little complicated. My dissatisfaction isn't large, but it *is* there. I'm still not a good prospect for a new word processor, but the inevitable seeds of change are germinating—dissatisfaction exists and it's likely to grow.

What will happen next? Most probably it will gradually become clear to me that the editing limitations are a real nuisance. I'll perceive significant problems and difficulties, not just a minor dissatisfaction. And at this point it will become very much easier for somebody to interest me in a new machine.

But my perception of a problem, even if the problem is severe, doesn't mean I'm ready to purchase. The final step in the development of a need is for the problem to be translated into a want, a desire, or an intention to act (Figure 3.2). I'm not going to buy a new word processor until I *want* to change. And when this happens, I'm ready to buy.

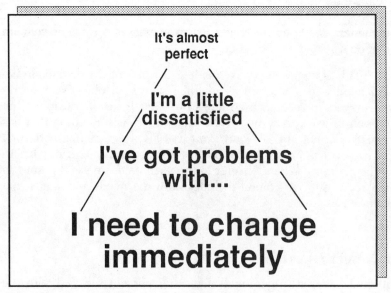

Figure 3.2. Developing needs.

So we can say that needs normally:

- Start with minor imperfections.
- Evolve into clear problems, difficulties, or dissatisfactions.
- Finally become wants, desires, or intentions to act.

In small sales, as we've seen, these stages can be almost instantaneous. In larger sales the process may take months or even years.

Implied and Explicit Needs

As we began to research customer needs at Huthwaite, we looked for a simple way to express this series of stages. We decided to divide needs up into two types (Figure 3.3):

Implied Needs. Statements by the customer of problems, difficulties, and dissatisfactions. Typical examples would be "Our present system

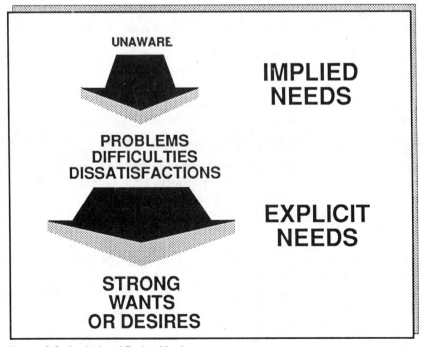

Figure 3.3. Implied and Explicit Needs.

can't cope with the throughput," "I'm unhappy about wastage rates," or "We're not satisfied with the speed of our existing process."

Explicit Needs. Specific customer statements of wants or desires. Typical examples would include "We need a faster system," "What we're looking for is a more reliable machine," or "I'd like to have a backup capability."

In this way we were able to take the continuum of needs and simplify it into just two classes, Implied and Explicit.

I'm always suspicious of people who introduce new jargon terms. If I'd been reading this chapter, I'd have asked myself questions like: What's the point of dividing needs up into Implied and Explicit? Doesn't it just introduce an unnecessary complication? How's it going to help me sell? These are fair questions, and they have an important answer. Our research suggests that in small sales the distinction between Implied and Explicit Needs isn't crucial for success. But in larger sales, one of the principal differences between very successful and less successful salespeople is this:

- Less successful people don't differentiate between Implied and Explicit Needs, so they treat them in exactly the same way.

- Very successful people, often without realizing they're doing so, treat Implied Needs in a very different way than Explicit Needs.

Let's look at some research evidence. In one of our studies we tracked 646 simple sales, counting how many times the customer stated an Implied Need during the call. Figure 3.4 shows the results. The successful calls contained more than twice as many Implied Needs as the unsuccessful calls. This suggests that, in simple sales, the more Implied Needs you can uncover, the better your chance of getting the business. Confirmation of this comes from another study that we carried out with a large office products company. The company was divided into two divisions, one selling simpler low-end products and one concerned with larger major sales. In the division selling low-end products, when a group of salespeople was trained to uncover more Implied Needs, its sales went up by 31 percent compared with those of an untrained control group. So it's fair to say that, at least in smaller sales, the more Implied Needs you can uncover, the greater your chances of success.

But what about larger sales? Is the same thing true there? No, it's not. As the sale becomes larger, the relationship between Implied Needs and success diminishes (Figure 3.5). In one of our studies, we analyzed 1406 larger sales, where the average contract size was $27,000. We found that—unlike small sales—there was no relationship between the number

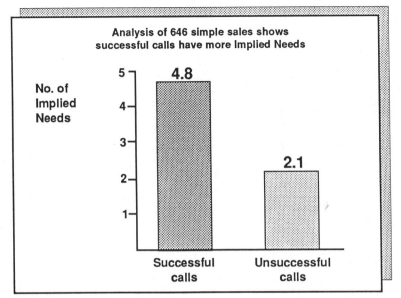

Figure 3.4. Implied Needs predict success in simple sales.

of Implied Needs the seller uncovered and the success of the call. Implied Needs are buying signals in small sales, but not in large.

What does this mean? Our interpretation is that, in larger sales, the sheer quantity of Implied Needs—or customer problems—that you uncover doesn't have much influence on the outcome of the call. Instead, Implied Needs are just a starting point, the raw material that successful salespeople use as part of their needs-development strategy. What matters in the larger sale isn't the number of Implied Needs you uncover, but what you do with them *after* you've uncovered them. As an example of this, in the high-end sales division of the office products company, we carried out a test whereby we were able to increase the sales of 49 people by 37 percent compared with a matched control group. Yet unlike their low-end colleagues, these salespeople's success was unrelated to the number of Implied Needs they uncovered.

Why Implied Needs Don't Predict Success in Larger Sales

When pocket calculators were first introduced, they were offered for sale at a trade show. There was an incredible response. The manufacturer, who had brought 1500 calculators to the booth, had sold every

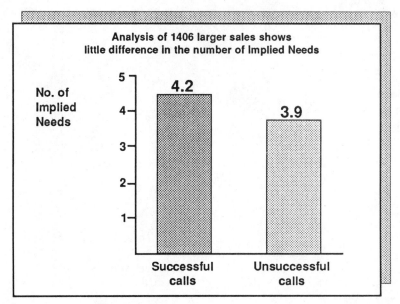

Figure 3.5. Implied Needs do not predict success in larger sales.

one in less than 2 hours. Hundreds of potential customers had to be turned away. Why was the new calculator so successful? Because it created instant dissatisfaction with the sheer bulk and inconvenience of large desk calculators. In other words, it generated an immediate Implied Need. But there was another equally important factor. The new calculator also represented a real price breakthrough, being less than one-fifth the cost of the cumbersome adding machines it was designed to replace. So visitors to the trade show had a twin incentive to purchase; they had Implied Needs (or dissatisfactions with their existing adding machines) and an amazingly low cost for the new replacement. Combine these two points and it's easy to see why people were lining up to buy.

But what would have happened if the new calculators had been 5 times the price of a mechanical adding machine instead of just one-fifth? Would there still have been the same rush to buy? Almost certainly not. The reason why the calculators were so attractive was that they offered such good *value*. In other words, they gave buyers a lot of capabilities for very little money.

Anyone making a decision to purchase must balance two opposing factors. One of these factors is the seriousness of the problems that the purchase would solve. The other is the cost of the solution. In the case of the calculators, as in many small sales, because the cost was so low it was easy for relatively superficial needs to tip the balance in favor of purchase.

The Value Equation

One way to think about the relationship between the size of needs and the cost of a solution is the concept of the value equation. As Figure 3.6 shows, if the customer perceives the problem to be larger than the cost of solving it, then there's probably a sale. On the other hand, if the problem is small and the cost high, then there's unlikely to be a purchase.

The price of a product or service is usually lower in simple sales. As a result, the size of the perceived needs on the other side of the equation doesn't have to be so great. That is, the Implied Needs may be quite sufficient to justify a purchase in the case of a small decision, such as buying the calculator. But if the calculator had cost *more* than conven-

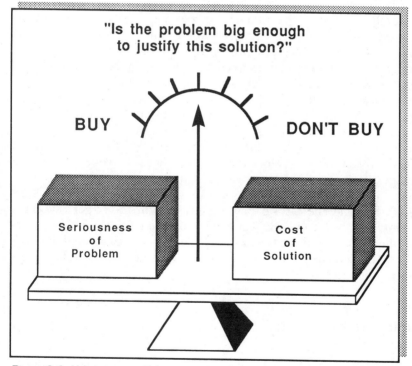

Figure 3.6. Value equation: If the seriousness of the problem outweighs the cost of solving it, there is a basis for a successful sale.

tional adding machines, then the need would have to be correspondingly bigger to justify a purchase.

This explains why you can sell successfully in smaller sales, where the cost of the solution is generally low, just by uncovering problems, or Implied Needs. And it also explains why, in major sales, you must develop the need further so that it becomes larger, more serious, and more acute in order to justify the additional cost of your solution. Remember that in larger sales the cost isn't measured only in terms of money. As I said earlier, a bad decision can cost the buyer's job. The buyer often perceives significant risks and hassles (which can't be measured in cash terms) as *adding* to the cost side of the value equation.

Explicit Needs and Success

If it's true that the need has to be bigger to justify a more costly solution, then you'd expect that success in larger sales might be much more closely related to the number of Explicit Needs in the call than to the number of Implied Needs. This is easy to test.

In the study of 1406 larger sales that I cited earlier, we also recorded the number of times the customer expressed an Explicit Need—which you'll remember is a specific statement of a want or desire that the seller's product can satisfy. As Figure 3.5 showed, the Implied Needs were not significantly higher in the successful calls. As Figure 3.7 shows, however, the Explicit Needs were twice as high in the calls that succeeded. This data confirms that, as the sale grows larger, it becomes increasingly important to obtain Explicit Needs, not just Implied Needs.

So, in larger sales, Implied Needs don't predict success, but Explicit Needs do. In smaller sales, both Implied Needs and Explicit Needs are success predictors. What does this mean in terms of your questioning strategy? In the smaller sale, a strategy that uncovers problems (Implied Needs) and then offers solutions can be very effective. In larger sales this is no longer the case. A probing strategy for the larger sale must certainly start by uncovering Implied Needs, but it can't stop there. Successful questioning in the larger sale depends, more than anything else, on how Implied Needs are developed—how they are converted by questions into Explicit Needs.

Buying Signals in the Major Sale

Most people in selling are familiar with the concept of *buying signals,* statements made by the customer that indicate a readiness to buy or to

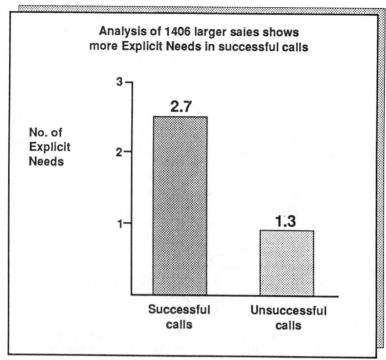

Figure 3.7. Explicit Needs and success in larger sales.

move ahead. Implied Needs are accurate buying signals for small sales; the more times a customer agrees to a problem or difficulty, the more likely the sale. In contrast, Explicit Needs are the buying signals that predict success in larger sales. We've observed that as salespeople grow more experienced, they usually give more weight to Explicit Needs as buying signals in judging how successful a call has been. Less experienced people put too much weight on Implied Needs.

For example, here's an inexperienced seller in the telecommunications industry. Notice how he puts great emphasis on the Implied Needs he has uncovered as evidence that the sale has advanced.

INTERVIEWER: ...so you'd say the call was successful?

SELLER: Yes, I think so.

INTERVIEWER: Was there anything the customer said—buying signals, for instance—that made you feel it was a success?

SELLER: Yes. He agreed that he had a capacity problem during morning peaks.

INTERVIEWER: Anything else?

SELLER: He's not happy about the quality of the data transmission.

INTERVIEWER: And on the basis of these "signals," you'd say that it's been a successful call?

SELLER: I think so. After all, we can help him with both of those problems. I'd think there's a good chance of some business.

Here, the seller judges the call as successful because the customer raised two problems, or Implied Needs. But as discussed earlier, there's no relationship between the number of problems you uncover in a large sale and whether the customer will ultimately buy from you. In this case the seller was surprised and disappointed to find, 2 weeks later, that the customer was talking to a competitor who, a few months later, successfully took the business.

In contrast, let's hear how a very successful seller from the same sales organization judges call success. She's one of the top five performers in her region, which contains over 400 salespeople.

INTERVIEWER: Was this a successful call?

SELLER: Difficult to tell. I found a few problems we could solve, but until I've had a chance to go back and develop them more, I'd prefer to hold judgment on whether we're going to get anywhere.

INTERVIEWER: Does that mean you don't see the problems you uncovered as "buying signals"?

SELLER: Indirectly they are, I guess. After all, you don't get anywhere unless you find some problems you can handle. So no problems means no sale—and that's a kind of negative signal—those are the worst calls. But I wouldn't really say that problems are positive buying signals.

INTERVIEWER: In general, what *are* the buying signals that tell you a call's successful?

SELLER: It's when you hear the customer talking about *action*. Things like "I'm going to overhaul our data network next year" or "We're looking for a system with these three characteristics." It's things like that.

INTERVIEWER: You know about the difference between Implied and Explicit Needs. It sounds like you're saying that Explicit Needs are a better signal than Implied Needs. Would that be right?

SELLER: Yes. You can't just rely on problems, you've got to have something stronger. That's why I think that the big skill in selling isn't so much getting the customer to admit to problems. Almost everyone I call on has problems, but that doesn't mean they'll buy. The real skill is how you grow those problems big enough to get action. And when the customer starts talking about action, that's when I hear "buying signals."

Here, unlike the inexperienced person, the seller puts little faith in problems or Implied Needs. Instead, her focus is on what she calls "actions." The examples she offers are what, in our terminology, we would call Explicit Needs. Like most of the very successful people we worked with, this seller puts strong emphasis on needs development as the most important selling skill.

I suggested in Chapter 2 that developing needs is the key function of questions. In terms of the larger sale, we can now express this more precisely:

The purpose of questions in the larger sale is to uncover Implied Needs and to develop them into Explicit Needs.

In the next chapter I'll show how this can be done using the SPIN questions.

4

The SPIN Strategy

Chapter 3 concluded that the purpose of questions in a sales call is to uncover Implied Needs and to develop them into Explicit Needs. In this chapter we'll be looking at how the four SPIN questions—Situation, Problem, Implication, and Need-payoff—can each be used to help this needs-development process.

Situation Questions

In our research at Huthwaite we found that very early in the sales call, particularly with new accounts or new customers, salespeople's questions tend to follow an identifiable pattern. Suppose, for example, that you're calling on me for the first time. What questions would you ask? You might want to know something about *me,* so you'd ask questions like:

What's your position?

How long have you been here?

Do you make the purchasing decisions?

What do you see as your objectives in this area?

You might also want to know something about my business, so you might ask:

What sort of business do you run?

Is it growing or shrinking?

What's your annual sales volume?

How many people do you employ?

You would need to understand how my business was operating, so you might ask questions like:

What equipment are you using at present?

How long have you had it?

Is it purchased or leased?

How many people use it?

What's the common factor in all these questions? Each one collects facts, information, and background data about the customer's existing situation. So we gave them the obvious name, Situation Questions (Figure 4.1).

Situation Questions are an essential part of most sales calls, particularly those calls made early in the selling cycle. What did our research uncover about them?

- Situation Questions are not positively related to success. In calls that succeed, sellers ask fewer Situation Questions than in calls that fail.

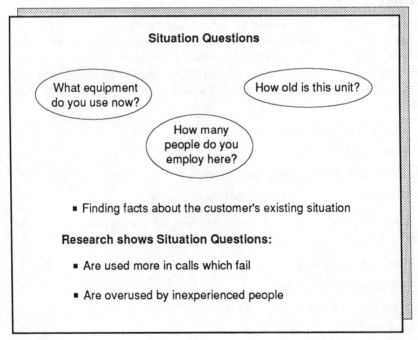

Figure 4.1. Situation Questions.

- Inexperienced salespeople ask more Situation Questions than do those who have longer sales experience.

- Situation Questions are an essential part of questioning, but they must be used carefully. Successful salespeople ask fewer Situation Questions. Each one they ask has a focus, or purpose.

- Buyers quickly become bored or impatient if asked too many Situation Questions.

These findings are easy to explain. Ask yourself who benefits from Situation Questions, the buyer or the seller? Clearly it's the seller. A busy customer doesn't generally derive great delight and happiness from giving a salesperson detail after detail of his or her situation. And this is especially true of professional buyers and purchasing agents. I once worked for several weeks with buyers from British Petroleum's central purchasing function. Even in my neutral role as an observer, I groaned inwardly when seller after seller asked questions like "Tell me about your business" or "What steps do you go through in making a purchasing decision here?" I don't know how the buyers stayed sane, patiently answering the same questions day after day. I've come to believe that there's a special place in hell reserved for wicked salespeople where they sit for all eternity being forced to answer their own Situation Questions.

Why do we find that inexperienced salespeople ask more Situation Questions than those with greater selling experience ask? Presumably it's because Situation Questions are easy to ask and they feel safe. When I didn't know much about selling, my main concern in the call was to be sure I didn't offend the buyer. And because Situation Questions seemed so inoffensive, I asked a lot too many of them. Unfortunately, in those days, I hadn't hit on the great sales truth that you can't bore your customers into buying. And the fault with Situation Questions is that, from the buyer's point of view, they *are* likely to be boring.

Does this mean that you shouldn't ask Situation Questions? No—you can't sell without them. What the research shows is that successful people don't ask *unnecessary* Situation Questions. They do their homework before the call and, through good pre-call planning, eliminate many of the fact-finding questions that can bore the buyer.

As sellers become more experienced, their behavior changes. They no longer spend most of the call collecting background situation information. Instead, their questions move to a different area.

Problem Questions

Experienced salespeople are most likely to ask questions like these:

Are you satisfied with your present equipment?

What are the disadvantages of the way you're handling this now?

Isn't it difficult to process peak loads with your present system?

Does this old machine give you reliability problems?

What's the common factor in all these questions? Each one probes for problems, difficulties, or dissatisfactions. Each invites the customer to state Implied Needs. We called them Problem Questions (Figure 4.2), and our research found that:

- Problem Questions are more strongly linked to sales success than Situation Questions are.

- In smaller sales the link is very strong: the more Problem Questions the seller asks, the greater the chances that the call will be successful.

- In larger sales, however, Problem Questions are not strongly linked to sales success. There's no evidence that by increasing your Problem Questions you can increase your sales effectiveness.

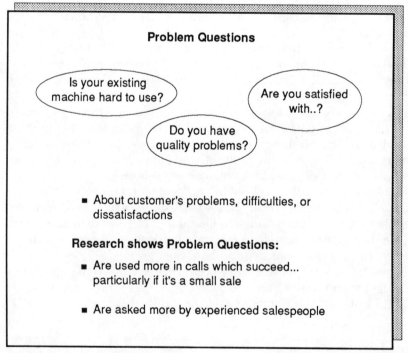

Figure 4.2. Problem Questions.

- The ratio of Situation to Problem Questions asked by salespeople is a function of their experience. Experienced people ask a higher proportion of Problem Questions.

Let's look more closely at what these findings mean. It's hardly surprising that Problem Questions have a more positive effect on customers than Situation Questions do. If you can't solve a problem for your customer, then there's no basis for a sale. But if you uncover problems you can solve, then you're potentially providing the buyer with something useful.

Problem Questions and Experience

It's also easy to understand why experienced people ask fewer Situation Questions and more Problem Questions. I can remember how this happened in my own selling—possibly you've similar memories. When I was young and inexperienced, my typical sales call consisted of as many Situation Questions as the buyer would let me ask. Then, when the inevitable glazed expression crossed the buyer's face, usually followed quickly by signs of impatience, I'd stop questioning and begin to talk features of what I had to offer. If at that point in my career you'd told me to ask about the buyer's problems, I would have been reluctant. Even the "safe" Situation Questions were making my buyers impatient—I certainly didn't want to risk upsetting them further with potentially offensive questions about problems.

But the day came when I screwed up my courage and began to ask about problems. To my surprise, instead of being offended, customers started to sit up and take notice. My calls improved. Soon I was spending more and more of the call asking about problems and less time uncovering interminable details of the situation. Most experienced people I've talked to can remember a very similar transition in their own selling.

Problem Questions in the
Larger Sale

It's true that Problem Questions are more strongly related to success in smaller sales, but they're nevertheless an essential part of effective probing as the sale grows larger. After all, if you can't uncover any problems to solve, you don't have a basis for a business relationship. In major sales there are, as we'll see in this chapter, other more powerful types of questions. But it's Problem Questions that provide the raw material on which the rest of the sale will be built. When we're coaching major-account salespeople, our starting point is most likely to be an analysis of how they are asking Problem Questions.

A Harder Question

Why should Problem Questions be so much more powerful in smaller sales than in large? Let's look at the research evidence. As Figure 4.3 shows, in our analysis of 646 smaller sales we found that the level of Problem Questions was twice as high in calls that succeeded. And as described in Chapter 3, when we trained people selling cheaper goods to ask more Problem Questions, there was a significant increase in their sales.

However, Problem Questions are much less strongly linked to success in larger sales (Figure 4.4). This is because Implied Needs, as we saw in Chapter 3, don't predict success in large sales. The purpose of Problem Questions is to uncover Implied Needs. So if Implied Needs don't predict success in the larger sale, neither should Problem Questions.

An Interesting Exception

Although Problem Questions are generally more powerful in small sales than in large, there's one interesting exception. Masaaki Imai, president

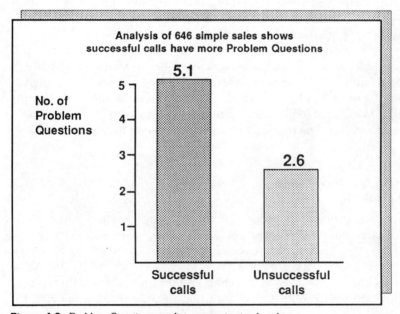

Figure 4.3. Problem Questions predict success in simple sales.

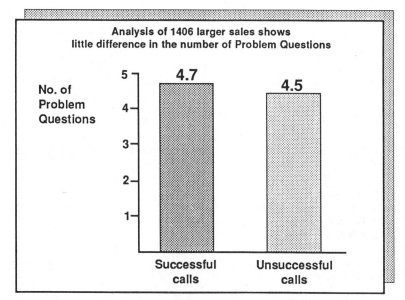

Figure 4.4. Problem Questions do not predict success in larger sales.

of the Cambridge Corporation, carried out some experiments with us in Japan. While it's quite acceptable in the west for sellers to ask buyers about problems, this isn't so easy in the Japanese culture. There's always the risk of being insulting or offensive if you suggest that your customer—a person of status—has problems. Because of this cultural difference, Japanese salespeople ask very few Problem Questions compared with their western counterparts. But even though Problem Questions may be harder to ask, is there any evidence that they link to sales success in Japan?

Working with the Engineering Products Division of Fuji Xerox, Imai found that despite the barriers to asking them, Problem Questions were indeed higher in successful calls. When a group of salespeople was trained in probing skills that included Problem Questions, its sales rose by 74 percent compared with an untrained control group. In this case, Problem Questions were powerfully linked to success in a large sale.

Implication Questions

Most experienced salespeople, put in front of a major-account customer, are able to do an adequate job of asking Situation and Problem Questions. Unfortunately, this is where most people's probing stops. In small sales you can be very successful if you uncover problems and then demonstrate that you can solve them—so a selling style based only on Situation and Problem Questions can be very effective. However, even though many people use this style in larger sales, it isn't effective in the larger sales. This small example should illustrate why:

> SELLER: *(Situation Question)* Do you use Contortomat machines in this division?
>
> BUYER: Yes, we've got three of them.
>
> SELLER: *(Problem Question)* And are they difficult for your operators to use?
>
> BUYER: *(Implied Need)* They *are* rather hard, but we've learned how to get them working.
>
> SELLER: *(offering a solution)* We could solve that operating difficulty for you with our new Easiflo system.
>
> BUYER: What does your system cost?
>
> SELLER: The basic system is about $120,000 and...
>
> BUYER: *(amazed)* $120,000!!! Just to make a machine easier to use! You must be kidding.

What's happened here? The buyer perceives a small Implied Need— "They *are* rather hard"—but certainly doesn't see that the problem justifies a $120,000 solution. In terms of the value equation (Figure 4.5), the problem isn't big enough to balance the high cost of solving it. But what if the price of the Easiflo system had been just $120 instead of $120,000? Would the buyer have reacted so negatively? Probably not; while $120,000 is outrageous, $120 is a small price to pay for ease of use. So if this had been a small sale—if the Easiflo product had cost a mere $120—then just uncovering the Implied Need that the existing machines were hard to use might have been enough to get the business. As we saw in Chapter 3, Implied Needs do strongly predict success in smaller sales.

In larger sales, however, it's clearly not sufficient to uncover problems and offer solutions. What *should* the seller have done? It's here that Implication Questions become so important to success. Let's see how a more skilled seller would have used Implication Questions to develop the seriousness of the problem before offering a solution:

> SELLER: *(Problem Question)* And are they difficult for your operators to use?
>
> BUYER: *(Implied Need)* They *are* rather hard, but we've learned how to get them working.
>
> SELLER: *(Implication Question)* You say they're hard to use. What effect does this have on your output?
>
> BUYER: *(perceiving the problem as small)* Very little, because we've specially trained three people who know how to use them.

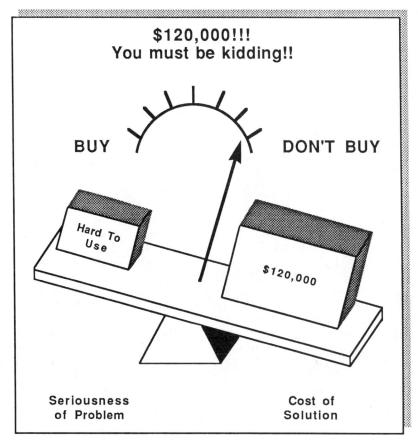

Figure 4.5

SELLER: *(Implication Question)* If you've only got three people who can use them, doesn't that create work bottlenecks?

BUYER: *(still seeing the problem as unimportant)* No, it's only when a Contortomat operator leaves that we have trouble while we're waiting for a replacement to be trained.

SELLER: *(Implication Question)* It sounds like the difficulty of using these machines may be leading to a turnover problem with the operators you've trained. Is that right?

BUYER: *(recognizing a bigger problem)* Yes, people certainly don't like using the Contortomat machines, and operators generally don't stay with us for long.

SELLER: *(Implication Question)* What does this turnover mean in terms of training cost?

BUYER: *(seeing more)* It takes a couple of months before an operator gets proficient, so that's maybe $4000 in wages and benefits for each operator. On top of that we pay Contortomat $500 to put new operators through off-site training in their Southampton plant. So add perhaps $1000 for travel costs. You know, that's about $5000 for each operator we train—and I guess we must have trained at least five this year already.

SELLER: So that's more than $25,000 in training costs in less than 6 months. *(Implication Question)* If you've trained five people in 6 months, it sounds like you've never had three fully competent operators at any time: how much production loss has this led to?

BUYER: Not much. Whenever there's been a bottleneck, we've persuaded the other operators to work overtime, or we've sent work outside.

SELLER: *(Implication Question)* Doesn't the overtime add even more to your costs?

BUYER: *(realizing the problem is quite serious)* Yes, we've been paying overtime at two and a half times the normal job rate. Even with the additional pay, the operators aren't very willing to work the extra hours—which I'm sure is one of the reasons we're getting such high turnover.

SELLER: *(Implication Question)* I can see how sending the work outside must also increase your costs, but is that the only implication of sending work out? Is the quality of work affected, for example?

BUYER: That's what I'm most unhappy about. I can control the quality of everything we produce internally, but when anything goes outside I'm at the mercy of other people.

SELLER: *(Implication Question)* And presumably, being forced to send work outside also puts you at the mercy of other people's delivery schedules?

BUYER: Don't talk about it! I've just spent 3 hours on the phone chasing a late delivery.

SELLER: *(summarizing)* So from what you've said, because your Contortomat machines are so difficult to use, you've spent $25,000 in training costs this year and you're getting expensive operator turnover. You've bottlenecks in production, and these result in expensive overtime and force you to send jobs outside. But sending jobs outside isn't satisfactory, because you're losing quality and getting late deliveries.

BUYER: When you put it that way, those Contortomat machines are creating a very serious problem indeed.

What effect has the seller had on the buyer's value equation? A small problem has now grown so much larger—and so much more costly—that a $120,000 solution no longer seems unreasonable (Figure 4.6).

This is the central purpose of Implication Questions in larger sales. They take a problem that the buyer perceives to be small and build it up into a problem large enough to justify action. Of course, Implication Questions can work in smaller sales too. A few months ago I was talking with a friend about cars. The conversation went like this:

FRIEND: How's your car, Neil?

NEIL: Not too bad. It's getting a bit old, but it still gets me around.

FRIEND: So you're not thinking of a new car, then?

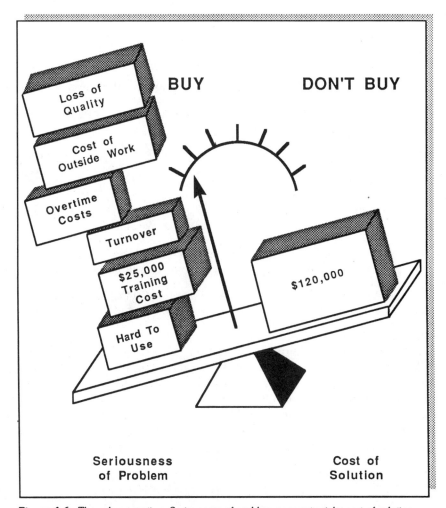

Figure 4.6. The value equation: Seriousness of problem now outweighs cost of solution.

NEIL: No. I can live a little longer with the one I've got.

FRIEND: *(Implication Question)* But your car must be at least 7 years old. Doesn't this mean that you can't claim any depreciation on it for business use?

NEIL: I suppose that's true.

FRIEND: *(Implication Question)* So you're losing a couple of thousand a year in tax write-offs?

NEIL: I'd not worked it out—I didn't think it would be that much—but you could be right.

FRIEND: *(Implication Question)* And doesn't a 7-year-old car mean that you're getting lousy mileage?

NEIL: It's true that I always seem to be filling it up. Yes, it never gave me good mileage—and lately it seems to be getting worse.

FRIEND: *(Implication Question)* And that's also leading to higher costs for you?

NEIL: Yes, it's expensive to run.

FRIEND: *(Implication Question)* And doesn't its age also mean a much higher oil consumption?

NEIL: You're right. I'm putting in a quart of oil every time I fill it—it's certainly more expensive to run than I'd like.

FRIEND: *(Implication Question)* What's the effect of age on your car's reliability?

NEIL: That *is* a worry. I've only had a couple of breakdowns, but…well, you know how it is, every time I start a journey I wonder whether I'm going to make it OK.

FRIEND: *(Implication Question)* And if it *does* break down, isn't it going to be increasingly hard to find a garage that stocks spares for a 7-year-old car?

NEIL: I've been lucky so far, but that's a good point.

FRIEND: *(Implication Question)* Wouldn't it be awkward for you if you broke down somewhere and had to wait 2 months for spares to be shipped?

NEIL: Yes, that's a worrying thought. You know, I'm beginning to wonder whether the time's come for me to change. What would you recommend in terms of a new medium-size car?

A car sale is certainly tiny in comparison to the larger sales we've been talking about. But as you can see, Implication Questions build up the size of Implied Needs in any decision (Figure 4.7). Even in very small one-call sales, Implication Questions are a good predictor of success. However, as we've seen, it *is* possible to be successful in small sales without Implication Questions. Because of this, some people might regard Implication Questions as unnecessary overkill when the decision size is small.

Professionals Often Sell Better than They Realize

There's another interesting thing about this car conversation. It wasn't a sales call; my friend knows nothing about selling. He's a consulting engineer who would run away in terror if you asked him to sell. Yet here he's doing a better job of developing my needs than 99 percent of the people whose job is to sell cars. Many professional people, particularly those who have to ask a lot of diagnostic questions as part of their work, can quickly and easily learn to use Implication Questions to help them sell.

At Huthwaite we've designed sales training for many professional and consulting organizations and we're continually surprised at how

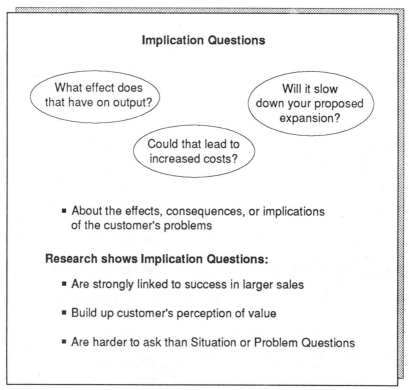

Figure 4.7. Implication Questions.

quickly many of those we train—who think of themselves as unable to sell—can become very skilled with Implication Questions. We're currently working with audit partners from one of the big eight accounting firms. Nothing could be further from the image of a successful seller than the stereotype most of us have of auditors. As the old saying goes, "Son, if you don't want the excitement and pressure of being an accountant, become an auditor." Some of the auditors we've trained seem to share this perception of themselves and are amazed to discover that many of the questions they ask as part of their normal professional conversation will also help them be successful in a selling role.

Where Implication Questions Work Best

Implication Questions are particularly powerful in certain types of sale. Obviously, as we've already seen, the main power of Implication Questions is in larger sales where it's necessary to increase the size of the problem in the customer's mind.

But our research also found that Implication Questions are especially powerful in selling to decision makers. It's often possible to achieve a positive outcome from calls on users or influencers simply by asking Problem Questions, but with calls on decision makers it's not as easy. Decision makers seem to respond most favorably to salespeople who uncover implications. Perhaps this is not surprising, for a decision maker is a person whose success depends on seeing beyond the immediate problem to the underlying effects and consequences. You could say that a decision maker deals in implications. There have been many occasions when we've been talking to decision makers after a call and heard them comment favorably on salespeople who asked them Implication Questions, saying things like "that person talked my language." Implications *are* the language of decision makers, and if you can talk their language, you'll influence them better.

A more curious research finding is that Implication Questions are particularly powerful in high-technology sales. It's one of those odd research findings that I don't know how to explain. One potential explanation is that in older, slower-moving technologies the customer may have been buying similar products for many years and so already understands the implications; consequently, Implication Questions are redundant. Somehow I don't find this explanation entirely convincing. My colleagues, who have worked extensively in high-tech markets, offer another explanation. Many high-tech customers, they suggest, perceive decisions as very risky because of the complex and rapidly changing high-tech marketplace. Under these circumstances, the customers have to see the problems with their present equipment as very severe before they feel ready to risk buying something they perceive to be new and different. I've also heard it suggested that customers mistrust high-tech salespeople, so they feel more comfortable with someone who holds back and tries to understand implications than they do with someone who jumps in with premature and often inappropriate solutions. The plausibility of this explanation is strengthened by the joke: What's the difference between people who sell used cars and people who sell high tech? Answer: People selling used cars *know* they are lying.

A Potential Negative

Implication Questions aren't a new discovery. People were asking them long before we began our research. Throughout history, effective persuaders have been uncovering problems and making them bigger by exploring their implications. Socrates was a master at doing this—read any of the Platonic dialogues and you'll see how one of the greatest persuaders of all time uses Implication Questions. However, the case of Socrates also illustrates that, despite their selling power, Implication Questions have a weakness. By definition, they make customers more uncomfortable with problems. Sellers who ask lots of Implication Questions may make their buyers feel negative or depressed. Not that many salespeople end up being forced to drink hemlock, but I do wonder whether Socrates's questioning behaviors contributed to his downfall.

Since making problems feel worse is both the strength and the potential danger of Implication Questions, is there some way to get the benefits of making a problem more acute without risking the penalties of depressing your customer? This is where the next type of question comes in.

Need-Payoff Questions

Our research at Huthwaite showed that successful people use two types of questions to develop Implied Needs into Explicit Needs. First they use Implication Questions to build up the problem so that it's perceived to be more serious, and then they turn to a second type of question to build up the value or usefulness of the solution. It's the use of this second type of question to build up the positive elements of a solution that prevents any unfavorable perception from customers. We call these positive solution-centered questions Need-payoff Questions (Figure 4.8). Basically, they ask about the value or usefulness of solving a problem. Typical examples include:

Is it important to you to solve this problem?

Why would you find this solution so useful?

Is there any other way this could help you?

What's the psychology of Need-payoff Questions? They achieve two things:

- They focus the customer's attention on the *solution* rather than on the problem. This helps create a positive problem-solving atmosphere where attention is given to solutions and actions, not just problems and difficulties.
- They get the customer telling *you* the benefits. For example, a Need-payoff Question like "How do you think a faster machine would help you?" might get a reply like "It would certainly take away the production bottleneck and it would also make better use of skilled operator time."

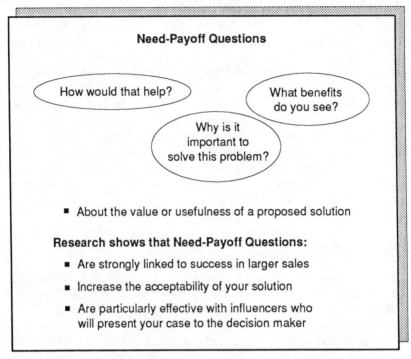

Figure 4.8. Need-payoff Questions.

Let's see how these objectives are achieved by looking at an extract from a sales call where the seller, whose product is a telephone system, is using Need-payoff Questions:

> SELLER: *(Need-payoff Question)*...so would you be interested in a way to control long-distance calls?
>
> BUYER: Well...yes, of course...but that's only one of the problems I have at the moment.
>
> SELLER: *(Need-payoff Question)* I'd like to consider those other problems in a minute. But first, you say you would like to control long-distance calling. Why is that important to you?
>
> BUYER: Well, right now I'm receiving a lot of pressure from the controller to contain my network costs. If I could reduce long-distance charges, it would sure help.
>
> SELLER: *(Need-payoff Question)* Would it help if you could restrict long-distance calling to authorized persons?
>
> BUYER: Well, yes...it would certainly prevent some of the excessive long-distance usage we're getting. Most of it's coming from unauthorized long-distance use.

SELLER: Can we go back to issues you raised about preparing phone-system management reports? *(Need-payoff Question)* May I assume you'd like improvement there also?

BUYER: Yes, it would be a big help.

SELLER: *(Need-payoff Question)* Is that because it would provide you with a better method for telephone cost accounting?

BUYER: Yes. You see, if we can identify departments that make calls, we can hold them accountable for their telephone charges.

SELLER: *(Need-payoff Question)* I see...is there any other way it might help?

BUYER: Umm...No. I think accountability is the main thing.

SELLER: *(Need-payoff Question)* Well that's certainly important...but don't you think it might also be important to know how long it takes to answer incoming calls and the total number of calls that go through each extension?

BUYER: That could be really useful.

SELLER: *(Need-payoff Question)* Useful for cost reasons, or is there something else?

BUYER: No, I wasn't thinking of costs. Where it would *really* help us is in improving customer service, and in this business that's important! Can you help us there?

SELLER: Yes, we can. Let me explain how our equipment will help to...

In this extract, Need-payoff Questions have succeeded in focusing customer attention on solutions rather than problems. Even more important, the customer begins to give benefits to the seller, saying things like "Where it would *really* help us is in improving customer service." It's no wonder our research found that calls with a high number of Need-payoff Questions were rated by customers as:

- Positive
- Constructive
- Helpful

Need-payoff questions create a positive effect. This is one reason why we found that Need-payoff Questions are particularly linked to success in sales that depend on maintaining a good relationship—such as sales to existing customers.

Need-Payoff Questions Reduce Objections

In a simple sale there's usually a straightforward relationship between your product and the problem it solves. It's possible for a solution to match the problem exactly. So, for example, a person worried about fire risks for important company papers might have a problem that could be solved perfectly by the purchase of a fireproof filing cabinet.

But as the sale grows larger, the fit between problem and solution generally becomes less straightforward. Problems in larger sales may have many parts, and the solution you offer the customer will deal with some of these parts better than with others. A problem such as low productivity, for example, may be caused by dozens of factors. When you present your solution, you run the risk that the customer will focus on the areas you *don't* solve rather than on those you do. When that happens, the customer may challenge your whole solution, as this example shows:

> SELLER: So your main problem is a high reject rate on the material you use for technical tests. Our new material is so easy to use that your technicians' reject rate would be reduced by approximately 20 percent.
>
> BUYER: *(raising objection)* Wait a minute. It's not only the test material that creates the reject rate. There are lots of other factors, such as processor temperature and developer oxidation. No. Don't give me all this stuff about easy-to-use material.

What's happening here? The buyer is raising an objection because the seller's solution deals only with one facet of a complicated problem. By making claims for the product, the seller has prompted the customer to raise some of these other facets and to reject the point the seller is trying to make.

In larger sales, the problems you're trying to solve will almost always be made up of many components and causes. Therefore, because it's most unlikely that you (or any of your competitors) can provide the perfect solution that solves every part of a complex problem, it can be dangerous for you to point out how well you can solve the problem. By doing so you invite the customer to make an issue of all the parts that you can't solve. What's more, sophisticated business customers rarely expect your solution to be perfect. Rather, they want to know if you can deal with the most important elements of a problem at a reasonable cost.

So how can you gain the customer's acceptance that your solution is worthwhile, even though it may not solve every part of the problem? This is an area where you can use Need-payoff Questions. If you can get the customer to tell *you* the ways in which your solution will help, then you don't invite objections. Nobody likes being told what's good for his or her department or business—especially by an outsider. Customers react more positively if they are treated as the experts. By using Need-payoff Questions, you can get the customer to explain to you which elements of the problem your solution can solve. This approach reduces objections and makes your solution more acceptable, as the next example shows:

SELLER: So your main problem is a high reject rate on the material you use for technical tests. *(Need-payoff Question)* And from what you've said, you'd be interested in anything that can cut this reject rate down?

BUYER: Oh yes. It's a big problem and we've got to take action.

SELLER: *(Need-payoff Question)* Suppose you had a material that was easier for your technicians to use, would this help?

BUYER: It would be one factor. But remember that there are lots of other factors, such as processor temperature and developer oxidation.

SELLER: Yes, I understand that there are several factors, and as you say, an easier material is one of them. *(Need-payoff Question)* Would you explain how having an easier material would help you?

BUYER: Well, it would certainly cut some of the rejects we're getting during the exposure stage.

SELLER: *(Need-payoff Question)* And that would be worth doing?

BUYER: Probably. I don't know precisely how much is lost there. It might be enough to make some difference.

SELLER: *(Need-payoff Question)* Is there any other way that an easier material could help?

BUYER: Those neat cassettes of yours don't need an experienced technician to set them up. Maybe that would help. Yes...if we had a material that was so easy to handle that an assistant could set it up, then the technician could spend more time on the processing stages, which could make a big impact on some of the processor problems we're getting. Hey, I like it.

In this example, the seller's use of Need-payoff Questions has allowed the *buyer* to explain the payoff and, as a result, to find the solution more acceptable.

Need-Payoff Questions Rehearse the Customer for Internal Selling

In smaller sales your success rests on how effectively you can convince the person you sell to, but this is not always the case in larger sales. As the size of the decision grows, more people become involved. Your success may often depend not just on how *you* sell, but on how well the people in the account sell to each other. In the small sale you're usually there during the whole sales process. But in larger sales there are likely to be many "sales calls" where influencers and users sell internally on your behalf and where there's no opportunity for you to be present.

A very experienced and successful sales manager in the process control industry was once asked to explain at a company conference how he had succeeded in selling a multimillion-dollar system to a major oil company. He said, "The most important thing to remember about really big sales is that you only play a small part in the selling. The real selling goes on in the account when you're not there—when the people *you* sold to go back and try to convince the others. I'm certain that the reason I succeeded was because I spent a lot of time trying to make sure that the people I talked to knew how to sell for me. I was like the director of a play. My work was during rehearsals: I wasn't on stage during the performance. Too many people in selling want to be great actors. My advice is that if you want to make really big sales, you've got to realize that even if you're a great performer, you won't be on stage for more than a fraction of the selling time. Unless you rehearse the rest of the cast, the show will be a flop."

Most people with experience in major-account selling would agree with this analysis. It's obvious that a lot of selling goes on when you're not around, so the better you prepare your internal sponsors, the easier it will be for them to convince others in the account. The problem is how: what's the best way to rehearse customers so that they sell effectively for you? Here's an extract from a typical call on a buyer who, if convinced, will afterward be "selling" internally:

> SELLER: …and another way the system will help you is in reduction of inventory levels.
> BUYER: Good. That's something we need to do. I'll be talking to the V.P. of Finance tomorrow and I'll mention this to him.
> SELLER: Be sure you tell him that we have automatic audit tagging.
> BUYER: Audit what?
> SELLER: It's a powerful new way to document and retrieve inventory records.
> BUYER: Uh…OK. I'll mention it.
> SELLER: Tell him that we cut inventory costs in Snitch Ltd. by 12 percent.
> BUYER: Because of this automatic audit thing?
> SELLER: Yes. And by controlling your seasonal peaks, we could do even better here. You'll let him know this, won't you?
> BUYER: Um…tomorrow may be a bad day for him…the meeting's about a downtown property issue. I'll see what I can do.

Even if this buyer does talk with the V.P. of Finance, how effective a piece of selling will it be? It will probably fail because the buyer clearly doesn't understand the product well enough to explain it.

Such insufficient understanding is not unusual. It's hard enough for salespeople to acquire all the technical and applications knowledge required to sell a sophisticated product or service. You can't expect the customer to understand in an hour something it's taken you months to learn yourself.

But if the customer isn't going to understand your product well enough to sell it effectively, what should you do? In an ideal world, of course, you would persuade the customer to take you along to every meeting. But in real life this just isn't practical. For one thing, the customer may be reluctant to lose control of the situation by giving you direct contact with top people. For another, it would be physically impossible for you to be present in every "sales" conversation that goes on inside an account. In a complex purchase, there may be dozens of conversations where your product is discussed between different people in the account. Even if the customer would let you, you couldn't possibly find time to attend every one of these discussions.

So there's no escaping the fact that in larger sales, a major part of the selling—perhaps most of it—will be done by your internal supporters while you're not there. This brings us back to the question of how you best prepare a customer to sell on your behalf, which is another area where Need-payoff Questions have a special use. In the next example, the seller uses Need-payoff Questions in a way that will help the buyer sell internally after the call is over:

> SELLER: …and another way the system will help you is in reduction of inventory levels.
>
> BUYER: Good. That's something we need to do. I'll be talking to the V.P. of Finance tomorrow and I'll mention this to him.
>
> SELLER: *(Need-payoff Question)* You say it's something you need to do. What benefits would you get from lower inventory levels?
>
> BUYER: Obviously the main one is cost.
>
> SELLER: *(Need-payoff Question)* Would cost be the most important benefit for your Finance V.P.?
>
> BUYER: Yes. Well…not necessarily. Now that I think about it, there could be another one that's more urgent. At tomorrow's meeting we're reviewing our downtown warehousing. We're using an expensive site, and our V.P. would like to close it and consolidate the inventory here. But we don't have quite enough warehousing space at this location. If your system could reduce levels at this site by just 5 percent, then we could close the downtown building.
>
> SELLER: *(Need-payoff Question)* And this would save you money?
>
> BUYER: About $250,000 a year. If you've got a way to help us do this, I'll try to get 15 minutes with our V.P. before the meeting.

Notice that in this example the seller uses Need-payoff Questions to get the buyer to describe Benefits. In doing this, the seller achieves several things:

- The buyer's attention is now focused on how the solution would help, not on product details as in the earlier example. I've said that buyers can't be expected to learn about your product in enough depth to explain it convincingly to others. But buyers *can* be expected to have an understanding of their own problems and needs. Need-payoff Questions concentrate on the area that buyers understand best: their own business—and how it would be helped by the solution you're proposing. When buyers talk to others in the account, it's in the area of needs, not of products, that they will be most convincing and will contribute most to your sales effort.

- The buyer is explaining the benefits to the seller, not vice versa. If you can get buyers to explain to you the value of your solution, it's good practice for when they come to give the same explanation to other people in the account. It's a much better rehearsal to get the buyer actively describing benefits to you than it would be for the buyer to listen passively while you describe the same benefits.

- When buyers feel that their ideas are part of the solution, they gain increased confidence in your product and feel an enthusiasm for it— the very qualities needed to sell the product for you when you're not present during the discussions.

In summary, Need-payoff Questions are important because they focus attention on solutions, not problems. And they make customers tell *you* the benefits. Need-payoff Questions are particularly powerful selling tools in the larger sale because they also increase the acceptability of your solution. Equally important, success in large sales depends on internal selling by customers on your behalf, and Need-payoff Questions are one of the best ways to rehearse the customer in presenting your solutions convincingly to others.

The Difference between Implication and Need-Payoff Questions

Both Implication and Need-payoff Questions develop Implied Needs into Explicit Needs, and because they have a similar purpose, it's easy to confuse them. Check whether you're clear about the difference between them by deciding which is which in this brief extract from a sales call:

Implication or Need-payoff Question?

1. SELLER: Does the slowness of your present system create bottlenecks in other areas of the process?   ☐

   BUYER: Yes, mostly in the preparation stage.

2. SELLER: And the preparation stage is an area you'd like to speed up?   ☐

BUYER: Yes, we're taking too much time right now in preparation.

3. SELLER: Because preparation is so labor-intensive, the excessive
time presumably means greatly increased costs?   □

BUYER: Unfortunately that's true.

4. SELLER: And what impact does this have on your competitiveness in a low-margin business like this one?   □

BUYER: It doesn't help.

5. SELLER: So what you'd like to see would be a reduction in prep-   □
aration costs?

BUYER: That would certainly make us more competitive.

6. SELLER: Is there any other way it would help you?   □

The Implication Questions are examples 1, 3, and 4. Examples 2, 5,
and 6 are Need-payoff Questions. Don't be too dismayed if you found it
difficult to decide which was which. At first, even the Huthwaite team
found it hard. In the early stages of our research, we would often come
across examples of questions where we weren't sure which category fit-
ted best. We'd write these examples up on a large white board in the
office. From time to time we'd meet to discuss these tough categoriza-
tion problems—*boundary issues* is the technical term—to make sure we
had the closely standardized agreement between us that's needed for
this kind of research.

During one of these discussions, the 8-year-old son of a team member
came into the office to collect his father from work. We were in the middle of a lengthy argument about the examples on the board, trying to
agree which were Implication and which were Need-payoff Questions.
The kid looked at the board for a moment and said, "That one, that
one, and that one are Implication Questions and all the others are
Need-payoff Questions." We were taken aback—we'd come to the same
conclusion but we'd needed half an hour to do it.

"How can you tell?" we asked.

"Easy," he said. "Implication Questions are always sad. Need-payoff
Questions are always happy."

He's right, and since then we've called it Quincy's Rule, after its 8-
year-old discoverer. Put in a more adult way, Implication Questions are
problem-centered—they make the problem more serious—and that's
why they are "sad." Need-payoff Questions, in contrast, are solution-
centered (Figure 4.9). They ask about the usefulness or value of solving

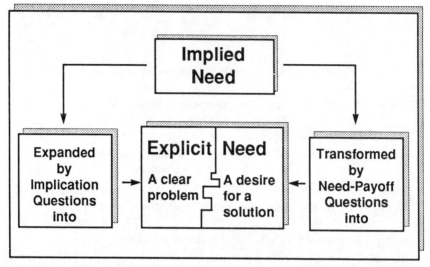

Figure 4.9. Implication Questions are problem-centered; Need-payoff Questions are solution-centered.

a problem, and that's why they seem "happy."

The senior management of our major clients might get the wrong impression if they knew that we'd been teaching their sales forces first to ask the sad questions, then to ask the happy questions—particularly if they knew an 8-year-old suggested the distinction. Consequently, we've never made Quincy's Rule public. But if you had trouble with the last examples, then try them again using Quincy's Rule. I think you'll agree that the Implication Questions (examples 1, 3, and 4) are sadder than the others.

Back to Open and Closed Questions

Near the end of Chapter 1, in the section "Questions and Success," I described the Huthwaite team's finding that the traditional open-and-closed model of questioning isn't related to effectiveness in larger sales. I'm sure that many readers, brought up on the sensible-sounding distinction between open and closed questions, must have found our conclusions hard to believe. I can now tell you a story that illustrates why the old open-and-closed distinction is less useful than it seems.

I was carrying out a study of sales management coaching in a large high-technology company. As part of this study, I traveled with salespeople and watched how they put coaching lessons into practice. One day I was traveling with an enthusiastic but inexperienced seller. During the call I recorded how often she used the different types of SPIN questions. My results, from our first call together, were:

Situation Questions	35
Problem Questions	0
Implication Questions	0
Need-payoff Questions	0

As we know, Situation Questions can become negatively related to success. The more you ask, the less likely it is that the call will succeed. Predictably, as the call progressed, the buyer first became bored, then became impatient, and finally asked us to leave. Afterward, as we rode down in the elevator, the seller asked me for advice. "I was trying to ask more open questions during this call," she explained. "Do you think I succeeded?" I was forced to reply that unless she asked about an area that had an impact on the customer—such as problems and their implications—it probably didn't make any difference whether her questions were open or closed. The sad truth is that a call which goes no further than Situation Questions is most unlikely to succeed. I imagine that there are tens of thousands of salespeople like her, struggling valiantly to understand unproductive distinctions between open and closed questions. If only she, and all those others, understood that the power of a question lies in whether it's asking about an area psychologically important to the customer—not whether it's open or closed.

The SPIN Model

Asking questions that are important to the customer is what makes the SPIN model so powerful. Its questioning sequence taps directly into the psychology of the buying process. As we've seen, buyers' needs move through a clear progression from Implied to Explicit. The SPIN questions provide a road map for the seller, guiding the call through the steps of need development until Explicit Needs have been reached (Figure 4.10). And the more Explicit Needs you can obtain from buyers, the more likely the call is to succeed.

Let's briefly review the whole SPIN Model and make a few observations about its use. Most importantly, please don't see SPIN as a rigid formula. It's not. Selling by a fixed formula is a sure recipe for failure in larger sales. Instead, see the model as a broad description of how successful salespeople probe. Treat it as a guideline, not a formula.

In summary, our research on questioning skills shows that successful salespeople use the following sequence:

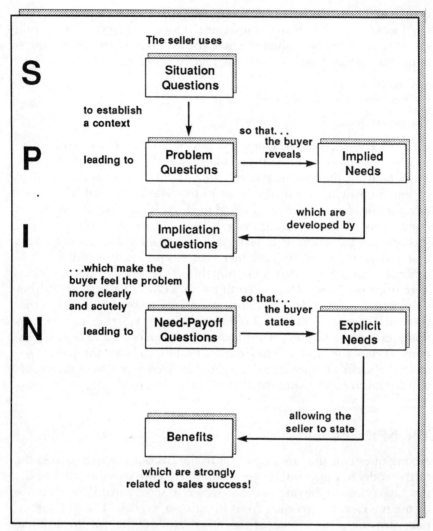

Figure 4.10. The SPIN Model.

1. Initially, they ask *Situation Questions* to establish background facts. But they don't ask too many, because Situation Questions can bore or irritate the buyer.

2. Next, they quickly move to *Problem Questions* to explore problems, difficulties, and dissatisfactions. By asking Problem Questions, they uncover the customer's Implied Needs.

3. In smaller sales it could be appropriate to offer solutions at this point, but in successful larger sales the seller holds back and asks *Im-*

plication Questions to make the Implied Needs larger and more urgent.

4. Then, once the buyer agrees that the problem is serious enough to justify action, successful salespeople ask *Need-payoff Questions* to encourage the buyer to focus on solutions and to describe the benefits that the solution would bring.

In a nutshell, this is the SPIN Model. Of course, it doesn't always work in quite this sequence. For example, if a customer begins a call by giving you an Explicit Need, you might go straight to Need-payoff Questions to get the buyer talking about how the benefits you could offer would help meet this need. Or sometimes, when you're exploring a problem or its implications, you may have to ask Situation Questions to give you more background facts. But in most calls the questioning naturally follows the SPIN sequence.

Many experienced salespeople, when introduced to the four simple questions, say, "I could have told you that without needing a million dollars of research. It's just obvious common sense." And, of course, they are right. We found this model by watching thousands of successful people sell. So it's not surprising that SPIN should make immediate and obvious sense to successful people. I don't like to describe the SPIN Model as some revolutionary discovery about how to sell. It's much better to think of it as the way most successful people sell on a good day when the call is going well.

Let me invite you to think of one of your most successful calls. Didn't it broadly follow the SPIN Model? Didn't you begin by finding out something about the customer's situation? So presumably you started out with Situation Questions. But fairly quickly you moved into discussion of a problem the customer had. How did you do this? By asking Problem Questions. Then, if you think of your most successful calls, you'll recall that as the customer talked, the problem seemed to get bigger and more urgent. Why did this happen? Presumably because you were developing the problem with Implication Questions. Finally, in your very best calls, were you telling the customer the benefits? Or was the customer getting excited and telling *you*, saying things like "Hey, *another* way you could help me would be..."? In most of my successful sales it's been the customer who was giving Benefits. And how did this happen? Because I used Need-payoff Questions—and I'm sure this is exactly what you've done in your successful calls too.

So you're probably using the SPIN Model already in your most effective sales. SPIN isn't new and unexpected. Its strength comes from putting a simple and precise description to a complex process. Consequently, it helps you see what you're doing well and helps you pinpoint areas where you need more practice.

How to Use SPIN Questions

To ask SPIN questions effectively, begin by recognizing that your role in a sales call is that of problem solver. Customer problems, or Implied Needs, are at the heart of every sale. Over the years I've helped my own selling enormously by clearly recognizing this simple fact. Before I go into a call, I ask myself, "What problems can I solve for this customer?" The clearer I can be about the problems I can solve, the easier it is to ask effective questions during the discussion.

Here is a simple technique to help you plan your call strategy and questions:

- Before the call, write down at least three potential problems which the buyer may have and which your products or services can solve.

- Then write down some examples of *actual Problem Questions* that you could ask to uncover each of the potential problems you've identified.

I'm not alone in finding it useful to list problem areas before each call. An experienced seller from a division of Kodak wrote me, "I've been selling for more than 20 years, and when you suggested making a list of problem areas before each visit, I thought the idea was too simple to be worth the effort. But I tried it and it's proved a very useful way to clarify my thinking and speed me successfully through the early stages of the sale." Many other people have found this simple suggestion helpful. Try it. In this way you'll uncover Implied Needs more quickly, and it will also help keep you from spending too much time asking unnecessary Situation Questions.

Most salespeople find Implication Questions harder to ask than either Situation or Problem Questions. In the average sales call we studied, only 1 out of every 20 questions asked was an Implication Question. It seems that, powerful though Implication Questions are, people have difficulty using them. Yet there's good evidence (see Appendix A if you're a doubter) that if you ask more Implication Questions, your calls will be more successful. What practical advice can we offer to help you use Implication Questions more often and more effectively? From our experience, the main reason why people ask so few of these important questions is that they don't plan them in advance. Here's a simple way to help you plan Implication Questions.

How to Plan Implication Questions

1. Write down a potential problem the customer is likely to have.

2. Then ask yourself what related difficulties this problem might lead

to, and write these down. Think of these difficulties as the implications of the problem—and be especially alert for those implications
which reveal the problem to be more severe than it may originally
have seemed.

As shown in Figure 4.11, for example, a seller planning a call has
identified "Existing machine is hard to use" as a potential problem
and has then thought of four related difficulties, one of which is that
there may be a shortage of qualified people to operate the machine.

3. For each difficulty, write down the questions it suggests. For instance, in Figure 4.11 the seller has noted that the shortage of qualified people suggests Implication Questions about overtime costs and
recruitment difficulties.

This is a very simple method, but it works well. Even the smartest
people we've studied find it hard to ask Implication Questions unless
they've planned them in advance. Whether you use our simple method
or a more elaborate one of your own, the basic principle is the same.
Good questions won't just spring into your mind while you're talking

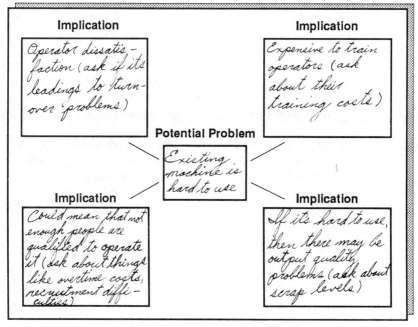

Figure 4.11. Planning Implication Questions.

with a customer. Unless you plan your questions in advance, you won't think of them during the call.

Using Need-Payoff Questions Effectively

Need-payoff Questions are so simple and so powerful that you'd expect them to be part of every sales call. No other type of question has so consistently positive an effect on the customer. Consequently, it's still a surprise to me that in almost half the calls we studied the sellers didn't use any Need-payoff Questions at all. It seems that, as with Implication Questions, people find them hard to ask. Even worse, when the average seller *does* use a Need-payoff Question it's often at the wrong point in the call. So let's look first at when *not* to ask Need-payoff Questions and then at how to increase our skills in asking them at the right point in the call.

Avoid Need-Payoff Questions Early in the Call.   Some people make the mistake of using Need-payoff Questions too early in the call, before they've identified the customer's problems. Paul Landauer of Abbott Laboratories tells the story of watching one of his salespeople open a call with the Need-payoff Question, "Mr. Customer, if I could show you something interesting, would you be interested?" In a less bizarre form, calls are often opened with questions like "If I could show you a way to increase productivity here, would you put my company on your bid list?" or "Would you be interested in a faster way to process your accounts?" These are Need-payoff Questions, but asked so early in the call, they are likely to put the customer on the defensive and thus be ineffective. The top performers we studied first built up needs before asking Need-payoff Questions. I'd advise you to do the same.

Avoid Need-Payoff Questions Where You Don't Have Answers.   Unfortunately, the only time when less effective salespeople will unfailingly ask Need-payoff Questions is at the worst possible point in the call. Take this example:

> CUSTOMER: *(Explicit Need)* I must have a machine that can give me double-sided copies.
>
> SELLER: *(whose machine can't copy on both sides)* Why do you need double-sided copies?
>
> CUSTOMER: *(explaining the need)* Because it will reduce my paper cost. And also, if we send double-sided copies through the mail, they're lighter, which cuts postage costs. There's another plus to double-sided copying too. It means we don't need so much filing space—and that's really important here.

The seller has asked a Need-payoff Question: "Why do you need double-sided copies?" It would be an excellent question if the seller were able to meet the need, because it encourages the customer to explain the benefits of double-sided copying. But for this seller, who can only offer single-sided copying, it's the worst possible question to ask. As a result of the Need-payoff Question, the customer's need grows stronger—and the seller can't meet it.

Most of us fall into this trap from time to time. We ask Need-payoff Questions for the needs we *can't* meet rather than for the needs we can. I'm sure you've asked the obvious question—"Why do you want to do *that?*"—when one of your customers has requested a capability you don't offer. The customer then responds to your question by telling you why the capability is important and, in so doing, strengthens the need for it.

The worst point to ask a Need-payoff Question is when the customer raises a need you can't meet. Conversely, the best point is when you *can* meet the need. Yet, ironically, this is when most people seem least likely to ask a Need-payoff Question. If the seller in the example above had a machine that offered double-sided copies, do you think she'd have asked the Need-payoff Question? Probably not. In our studies we found that when customers raised needs that the seller could meet, the most likely response from the seller was not to ask Need-payoff Questions but to begin talking about solutions.

Practicing Effective Need-Payoff Questions. Implication Questions require careful planning. You can't improve your skills with them unless you're prepared to invest a lot of patience and effort. At the same time, we've seen people dramatically increase their skills with Need-payoff Questions just by consolidating the idea with some straightforward practice exercises. Here's an example of a simple exercise that helps you practice Need-payoff Questions:

1. Get a friend or colleague to help you. The person you choose needn't know anything at all about selling. My son has been my "victim" for this exercise.
2. Choose a topic about a need that you believe the other person has. You might, for example, choose to talk about a new car, a vacation, a change of job, or—as in my son's case—a video camera.
3. Ask Need-payoff Questions to get the other person talking about the benefits of the topic under discussion. In my case, for example, I asked my son questions like these:

- Why do you think it would be good to have a video camera?
- What would it let us do that we can't do right now?

- Would anyone else in the family be pleased if we bought one?
- Do you think it would have any cost advantages compared with Super 8 film?

When you try this exercise, notice two things about it:

1. As in real life, it builds up noticeable enthusiasm in your "customer." A major-account seller from Xerox once told me that he tried out the exercise with a friend, using a new car as the topic. A week later she actually *bought* a new car, explaining to him, "Your questions really convinced me I should." The power of Need-payoff Questions is often visible in these simple practice demonstrations. Watch for it.
2. Unlike Implication Questions, which tend to be specific to a particular customer problem, Need-payoff Questions have wide generality. Many of the questions you'll use in this practice exercise are the same ones you can use in real calls. There are many generic Need-payoff Questions, such as these:

- Why is that important?
- How would that help?
- Would it be useful if...?
- Is there any other way this could help you?

Practice these first in safe situations like this exercise. Then try them in real calls. I think you'll be surprised at their effectiveness.

5

Giving Benefits
in Major Sales

We've seen in Chapter 4 how the SPIN Model provides a strong probing framework for the Investigating stage of the call. In this chapter, I want to show you what Huthwaite's research found about the Demonstrating Capability stage (Figure 5.1).

Features and Benefits: The Classic Ways to Demonstrate Capability

Sales training and books on selling have given a lot of attention to methods for Demonstrating Capability. Since the 1920s it's been recognized that some ways of presenting solutions to customers are more persua-

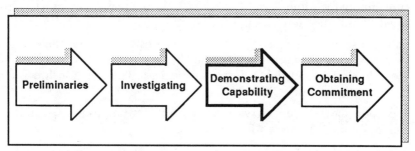

Figure 5.1. The Demonstrating Capability stage: Offering your solutions and capabilities to the customer.

sive than others. Anybody who has been through a sales-training program in the last 60 years is likely to have been taught the terms *Features* and *Benefits* as the two ways that you can describe your products or services. We're all so familiar with the concept that it scarcely seems necessary to explain that Features are facts about a product and are unpersuasive, whereas Benefits—which show how Features can help the customer—are a much more powerful way to describe your capabilities. If there was one area of selling where we expected our research merely to confirm the conventional wisdom, it was here with Features and Benefits.

But we were in for some surprises. Benefits, in the way you've probably been taught to use them, are ineffective in larger sales and are likely to create a negative response from the customer. And even something as simple as defining a Benefit is much harder than it seems. Before looking at our conclusions, let's begin by reviewing some basics.

Features

Everybody knows what Features are. They are facts, data, or information about your products or services. Typical examples of Features include "This system has 512K buffer storage," "There is a four-stage exposure control," and "Our consultants have a background in educational psychology." Features, as every writer has observed since the 1920s, are unpersuasive. Because they give neutral facts, they don't much help your sales presentation. On the other hand, the consensus of writers is that they don't harm you either.

What does our research show? From an analysis of the number of Features used in 18,000 sales calls, we found the following (Figure 5.2):

- Overall, the level of Features is slightly higher in unsuccessful calls (which, you'll remember, are those leading to Continuations and No-sales). But this difference is small enough for us to conclude that the conventional wisdom is right—Features are neutral. They don't help the call, but they don't harm it much either.

- In small sales there's a slight *positive* relationship between the use of Features and call success, so the calls higher in Features are slightly more likely to result in Orders or Advances. This relationship isn't true in larger sales.

- In larger sales, Features have a *negative* effect when used early in the call and a neutral effect when used later.

- Users respond more positively to Features than do decision makers.

- In the middle of very complex selling cycles of technical products, the

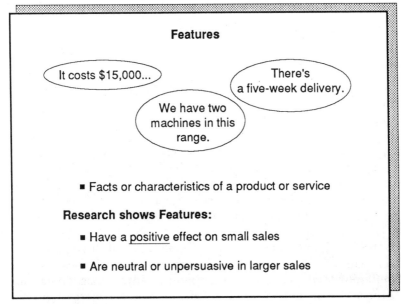

Figure 5.2. Features.

customer sometimes develops a "Features appetite." When this happens, the customer demands considerable product detail and may respond positively to Features. It's at this stage of the selling cycle that technical experts, systems analysts, and other sales-support people often have a positive impact on a customer.

We also found some curious relationships between the use of Features and the type of response from customers, which we'll explore more in the next chapter. But generally, our work on Features confirmed what writers have been saying for 50 years. Features are low-power statements that do little to help you sell. It's better to use Benefits than Features.

What's a Benefit?

Our problems started when we began to investigate Benefits. While everybody agrees on the definition of a Feature, no two writers on selling seem to have the same definition of a Benefit. Here are some of the many definitions that we uncovered from a miserable month spent reading every sales book and training program we could find:

A Benefit shows how a Feature can help a customer.

A Benefit must have a cost saving for the buyer.

A Benefit is any statement that meets a need.

A Benefit has to appeal to the personal ego needs of the buyer, not to organizational or departmental needs.

A Benefit must be something which you can offer and which your competitors can't.

A Benefit gives a buying motive.

There are more. Some definitions emphasize financial elements, and some concentrate on personal appeal. Others accept any elaboration of a Feature, such as explaining how it can be used. My personal favorite was from a sales manager in Honeywell who told me, "A Benefit is anything you say to a customer that's smarter than a Feature."

Which Definition Is Right?   How can we tell which of these definitions is better than the others? There's only one valid test: The best of these rival definitions is the one that has the most positive impact on customers. Is there one of these types of Benefits that occurs more often than others in successful calls? Our research team set out to test this by watching sales calls and counting how often the different types of Benefits were used in calls that succeeded and in calls that failed. After this initial testing of a half-dozen different definitions, we chose two for our major research test:

- *Type A Benefit.* This type shows how a product or service can be used or can help the customer.

- *Type B Benefit.* This type shows how a product or service meets an Explicit Need expressed by the customer.

We chose the Type A definition because it was the most common one used in the better sales-training programs. Most readers of this book will have been taught to use the Type A Benefit. In contrast, the Type B Benefit was our own definition. We chose it after watching hundreds of very effective salespeople in larger sales and analyzing the types of product statements they made to their customers.

At first sight, these two definitions of a Benefit seem very similar. However, their effect on customers is dramatically different, so it's worth examining how the two differ. For example, suppose I'm selling you a computer system and I say, "I assume you want a 32-bit system like our Suprox machine because, if you ever use graphics, it will be significantly faster for you." Have I made a Type A or a Type B statement? It can't be Type B, for I've *assumed* that you want faster graphics; you haven't actually expressed a need for graphics, let alone faster ones.

Take another example. You tell me that your present machine has a reliability problem. I reply, "Because our Suprox machine uses a new generation of high-reliability components, it could solve your present reliability problem." What kind of statement is this? This time you've certainly expressed a need. You've told me that your present machine is unreliable. But have you expressed an *Explicit* Need? No; telling me that your present machine has a reliability problem is an Implied Need (a problem, difficulty, or dissatisfaction). So my statement meets an Implied Need, not an Explicit Need. Once again, we should classify it as a Type A Benefit, not a Type B.

How Important Is the Difference?   In our research test we found that the Type A Benefit is quite strongly related to success in smaller sales but is only slightly related to success in larger sales. (We'll see why later in this chapter.) In contrast, the Type B Benefit is very strongly related to success in all sizes of sales.

I don't know about you, but personally I find it hard to remember which is which whenever anything is labeled A or B. I wasn't the only one who found it confusing to refer to Type A and Type B Benefits, so we soon decided that it would be better to avoid further difficulties by putting more descriptive names in place of A and B. *We called the Type A Benefit an "Advantage." And for the Type B Benefit, because it was so strongly related to success, we kept the name "Benefit."*

Thus, what emerged from our research are three kinds of statements (or behaviors) that you can use to demonstrate capability, as shown in Figure 5.3. It's important to remember that if you've been through sales training in the last 20 years, you've probably been taught to use a lot of Type A Benefits—or Advantages. But as you can see in Figures 5.3 and 5.4, Advantages are more powerful in simpler sales than they are in the larger sales that are the subject of this book.

Almost certainly, you'll experience some confusion between the definition of Benefit that we're using here and the definitions you've learned in the past. Most salespeople I've worked with hate quibbling about definitions, and I don't blame them. But in this case, definitions are vitally important. For example, the Motorola Canada productivity study described in Appendix A shows that salespeople who used Benefits rather than Advantages increased their dollar volume of sales by 27 percent. That's more than a quibble. When the definition is derived from choosing the statements that have the highest impact on customers, then we're not just playing with words. Because the differences between Features, Advantages, and Benefits are so important, I'd like to

Behavior	Definition	Impact	
		On small sales	On larger sales
Features	Describe facts, data, product characteristics	Slightly positive	Neutral or slightly negative
Advantages (Type A Benefits)	Show how products, services, or their Features can be used or can help the customer	Positive	Slightly positive
Benefits (Type B Benefits)	Show how products or services meet Explicit Needs expressed by the customer	Very positive	Very positive

Figure 5.3. Features, Advantages, and Benefits.

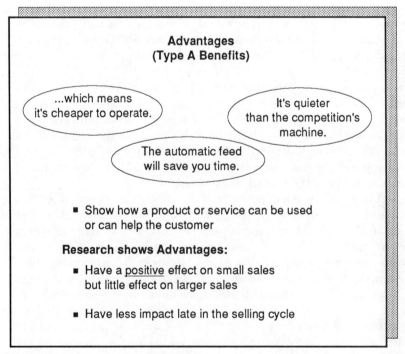

Figure 5.4. Advantages (Type A Benefits).

give you a chance to test your understanding of them by working through the following short transcript. See if you can pick out which of the 10 product statements offer Features, Advantages, or Benefits. Then check your answers against the ones given at the end of this chapter.

Types of Product Statements

		Is it a Feature, Advantage, or Benefit?
1. SELLER:	And another thing about the system is that it has balanced voltage stabilization.	☐
BUYER:	Oh, what does that do?	
2. SELLER:	It protects you from current surges so that you won't lose valuable data if you have a voltage fluctuation.	☐
BUYER:	That isn't necessary here. This building is wired for scientific use, so there's inbuilt voltage protection.	
3. SELLER:	But I'm sure you'll find the backup memory useful. It means that even in the event of an operator error wiping out your main files, you'll always have automatic backup—so you'll never run the risk of losing key data.	☐
BUYER:	And how much does this configuration cost?	
4. SELLER:	The basic core system costs $78,000.	☐
BUYER:	And is it compatible with our optical readers? I need to be able to read source data straight into memory.	
5. SELLER:	Yes, you'll be able to read your present data without any conversion, so if you want to read directly into memory you'll be able to do that.	☐
BUYER:	That's good. How about error rates? I must have less than 1 in 100,000.	
6. SELLER:	Then you'll be glad to hear that the system has one of the lowest error rates on the market—less than 1 in 1,500,000—which easily meets your need.	☐
BUYER:	Fine.	
7. SELLER:	And because of the low error rate, you can also use the system to rerun and verify data from your other processing sources—thus saving you the cost of a separate verification process.	☐
BUYER:	I'm not sure about that. We have other security issues around data verification, which means we wouldn't be permitted to take data from our other sources.	

*Is it a
Feature,
Advantage,
or Benefit*

8. SELLER: On the subject of security, this system has eight levels   ☐
             of possible coding built in.

    BUYER: Are they user-determined?

9. SELLER: On five levels. The other three are randomized or   ☐
             time-based.

    BUYER: Time-based?

10. SELLER: Oh yes. You see, the big plus of a time-based system   ☐
             for an organization like yours is that you can simul-
             taneously and automatically roll over access codes be-
             tween operating units—which means that your oper-
             ators don't have to memorize new codes, yet it's
             almost impossible for outsiders to break in.

Now that you're familiar with the rather special way we use the terms
Advantages and *Benefits,* let's examine the research evidence in more
detail.

The Relative Impacts of Features, Advantages, and Benefits

I've said that Advantages—statements showing how your product can
be used or can help the customer—have a much more positive impact
on small sales than on larger ones. Why? It seems odd that the impact
should be so much less in the large sale. The most probable answer goes
back to the points I made about simple sales in Chapter 4. Remember
that we showed how you could be very successful in smaller sales by using Situation and Problem Questions to uncover Implied Needs and
then offering solutions.

What would these solutions be in terms of Features, Advantages, and
Benefits? They can't be Benefits because, as we've seen, you can only
make a Benefit if you address an Explicit Need that the customer has
expressed. In this case the solutions are offered to Implied Needs, so
they must be either Features or Advantages. We've seen that offering
solutions to Implied Needs isn't effective in larger sales. So this use of
Features and Advantages, which can work perfectly well in a small sale,
is likely to be ineffective as the sale grows larger (Figure 5.5).

This explains why our research found that Benefits are so much
more powerful in larger sales. To make a Benefit, you must have an

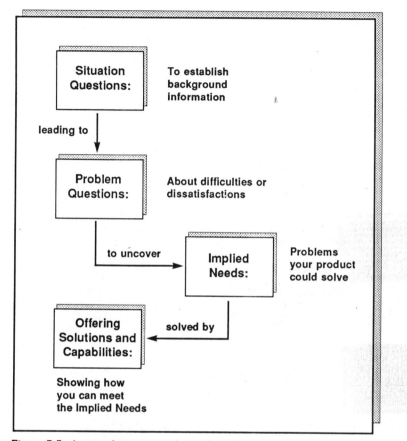

Figure 5.5. A recipe for success in the smaller sale, but for disaster in larger sales.

Explicit Need (Figure 5.6). But in order to get the Explicit Need, you normally must first develop it from an Implied Need by using Implication and Need-payoff Questions. Using Benefits, as we define them, can't be divorced from the way you develop needs. When my colleagues and I at Huthwaite run training programs, we are often asked for advice on how to use more Benefits. Our reply is simple: "Do a good job of developing Explicit Needs and the Benefits almost look after themselves." If you can get your customers to say, "I want it," it's not difficult to make a Benefit by replying, "We can give it to you."

Benefits and Call Success

One of our early studies that confirmed the power of Benefits was carried out in a number of high-technology companies across Europe and

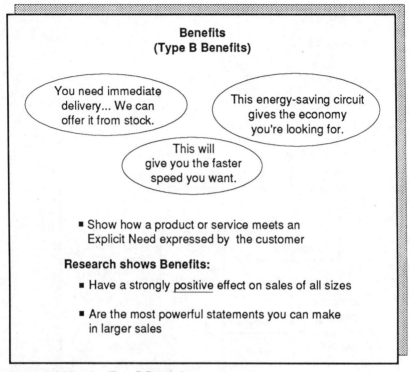

Figure 5.6. Benefits (Type B Benefits).

North America. We compared the level of Benefits in 5000 calls with the outcome of each call (Figure 5.7). We found that Benefits (and remember that our definition of a Benefit is a statement that shows how you can meet an *expressed Explicit Need*) were significantly higher in calls leading to Orders and Advances. In contrast, the level of Advantages (showing how your product can help or be used—what many of us have been taught to call "Benefits") was not significantly different in successful and unsuccessful calls.

Features, Advantages, and Benefits in the Longer Selling Cycle

One of the curious findings from our research was that the impacts of Features, Advantages, and Benefits on the customer are not similar throughout the selling cycle (Figure 5.8).

We were working with one of the world's leading business-machines companies, and part of our investigation involved measuring the effects

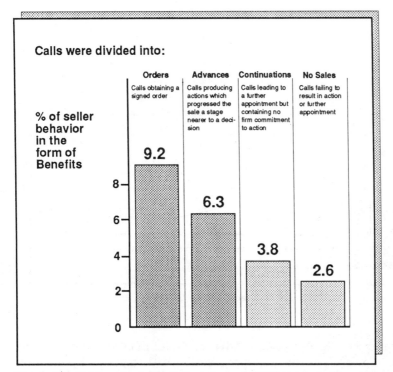

Figure 5.7. Relationship of Benefits to outcome in 5000 high-technology calls:
Chart shows relationship of Benefits to sales.

of sales behaviors at different points in the selling cycle. The average
selling cycle in this organization was 7.8 calls long. Company researchers, working with Huthwaite, accompanied salespeople into calls at different points in the cycle. They observed the frequency with which each
seller used Features, Advantages, and Benefits and then compared this
data with the outcome of each call. To be technical for a moment, the
vertical axis of the graph in Figure 5.8 actually shows the significance
level of each behavior measured by a battery of nonparametric tests. In
simpler terms, the higher a behavior comes on the vertical axis, the
more it's likely to help you sell.

As you can see in Figure 5.8, Features had a low impact on the customer throughout the selling cycle. Benefits, at the other extreme, had
a high impact whenever they were used. Advantages had an unusual behavior. We found that early in the cycle, particularly during the first
call, Advantages had a moderately good statistical relationship to call
success. This is another way of saying that Advantages had a positive
impact on the customer during the first call—sellers who used a lot of

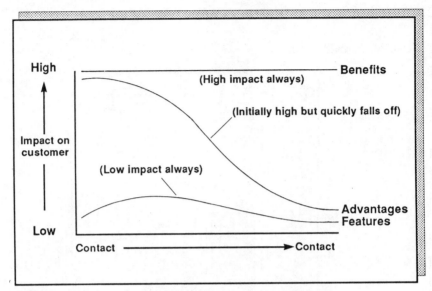

Figure 5.8. Features, Advantages, and Benefits across the selling cycle.

Advantages were likely to get an Advance rather than a Continuation or No-sale. However, as the cycle progressed, Advantages had a decreasing effect on the customer until, as the end of the cycle approached, they were no more powerful than Features.

Why Do Advantages Run Out of Steam?

To be honest, I'm not sure why Advantages are more effective early in the cycle than late. It's one of those findings which the Huthwaite research team still argues about whenever we get together. Possibly it's because, at a first meeting, the customer expects to hear about the product rather than to discuss needs. I'm sure you've often made first visits to customers who start off the call by saying "Now tell me all about this product of yours." I've certainly had customers who don't want to discuss needs until they know more about what I've got to offer.

Another possibility is that many of the sellers who jump in early with Advantages do so because they are genuinely enthusiastic about their products. They can't wait to start talking solutions. In the short term, their enthusiasm carries them along, at least to the point where the customer agrees to proceed to a further step in the selling cycle. However, if they continue a product-centered approach as the cycle progresses, they aren't responsive to customer needs and therefore become less effective.

A third possibility is that Advantages, as we've seen earlier, are very quickly forgotten after the call; Consequently, their effect is temporary. In contrast, Benefits continue to have an impact *between* calls because their link to Explicit Needs helps customers remember them.

Whatever the reason, I'm sure you've seen cases in your own company of this phenomenon in action. A typical example is the pushy, aggressive individual who's much more interested in selling the product than in meeting the customer's needs. This kind of person will frequently be very successful in the early stages of the sale. I'm sure you've listened, as I have, to the stories these people tell about how they've just had a first meeting with a new customer and impressed this customer mightily by the way they put the product across and showed how it could solve all the customer's problems. But how many of these promising beginnings turn into orders? Fewer than you'd expect. And a very likely reason is that the seller's high-Advantage style has helped early in the cycle but run out of steam as the sale progressed. But whatever the explanations, the research is giving us a simple but important message. Advantages are less powerful than Benefits all through the selling cycle. It never pays to offer an Advantage if you can go that bit further and offer a Benefit.

Selling New Products

There's one area of Demonstrating Capability that is generally handled badly, even by experienced salespeople. It happens to be an area vital to most organizations' success and it's a source of perennial frustration and disappointment to senior management. The area I'm talking about is the new-product launch. Over and over again, my Huthwaite colleagues and I are asked by top management to help explain why a new product has failed to meet its initial sales target.

"What's wrong?" they ask. "We were sure our projections were realistic. Yet now, 6 months into the launch, we're less than 50 percent of plan. Is it the product? Is it the sales force? What's going wrong?"

From the many product launches we've studied, one constant fact emerges. The biggest single cause of poor results early in a product's life can be explained in terms of Features, Advantages, and Benefits.

The Bells-and-Whistles Approach

When a product is new, how does product marketing generally communicate it to the sales force? The marketing people call the sellers together and tell them about what an exciting new product is coming. They explain all the Features and Advantages—all the bells and whistles. And what do the salespeople then do? They become excited about the product and go out to sell it. And when they are in front of customers, how do they behave? They communicate the product in exactly the same way it was communicated to them. Instead of asking questions to develop needs, they jump in with all the exciting Features and Advantages that the new product possesses.

Figure 5.9 shows the composite data from a number of product launches. As you can see, the average number of Features and Advantages given when selling new products is more than 3 times the level given by the same salespeople when selling existing products. The evidence suggests that the sellers' attention is much more on the product than on their customers. To be frank, I've done it myself—you've probably done the same thing too. Whenever Huthwaite launches a new product, we all get excited and enthusiastic, and we can't wait to tell our clients all about it. And like so many other companies, we wonder why—despite our enthusiasm—we're not making sales. We now understand that it's precisely *because* of our enthusiasm that we have a problem. Our enthusiasm has led us to become product-centered and to give Features and Advantages. As we've seen in this chapter, that's not an effective strategy for the major sale.

The Problem-Solving Approach

We had an interesting opportunity to test whether something as simple as excessive Features and Advantages could really account for the slow growth of new-product sales. A major company in a medical market invited us to carry out an experiment with the launch of one of its new products.

The product was a sophisticated, and expensive, piece of diagnostic equipment. It was clearly in the category of the larger sale. The machine was launched to most of the sales force in the conventional way—a high-key presentation of its Features and Advantages by the product marketing team. But we were allowed to launch it differently with a small experimental group of salespeople. Instead of showing them the product and describing its Features and Advantages, we didn't even let them see what they would be selling. "It's not important," we explained. "What *is* important is that this machine is designed to solve problems for the doctors who use it." We then listed the problems the machine solved and the needs it met. Finally, we had our group make a list of accounts where these problems could exist, together with the Problem, Implication, and Need-payoff Questions they would ask when they vis-

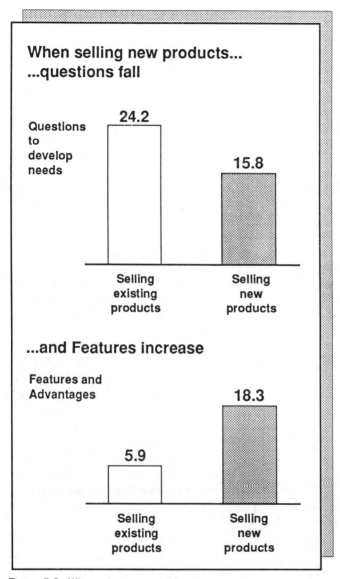

When selling new products...
...questions fall

Questions
to
develop
needs

24.2

15.8

Selling
existing
products

Selling
new
products

...and Features increase

Features and
Advantages

18.3

5.9

Selling
existing
products

Selling
new
products

Figure 5.9. When selling new products, the tendency is toward promoting the product, not on customer needs.

ited those accounts. By launching the product in terms of the problems it solved and how to probe for them, we were able to shift our small group's attention away from the product and back to customer needs. The proof that this was an effective strategy is in the sales results. Our group averaged a 54 percent higher level of sales than the rest of the sales force during the product's first year.

This research on new products also gave me an explanation for something that had puzzled me for many years. Some of the people with the best records for selling new products are the most cynical about product launches. I remember going to a product launch in Acapulco some years ago. The event was splendiferous. Big names from the entertainment world had been hired at unbelievable cost, and the place swarmed with public relations people, media specialists, communications consultants, and a variety of similarly expensive people. The salespeople, eagerly awaiting the great event, filed into the main hall to hear one of the most spectacular and costly Feature dumps of the decade. I was depressed at the enormous expense my client had gone to in order to make the sales force communicate the new product ineffectively, so I decided to wait outside until all the fuss and spectacle subsided. As I sat by the pool, I noticed two other people who had slipped out of the same presentation. Talking with them, I found that they were both very experienced high performers. "It's just another product," said one. "When the fuss dies down, I'll go back in and figure out which customers need it." Clearly he wasn't going to fall into the trap of neglecting needs in favor of Features and Advantages.

Have you ever noticed how, just when the new product is proving to be a disappointment and the sales force is losing its enthusiasm, sales suddenly start to improve? I recall exactly that happening when I was involved in the launch of a large new copying machine. At the time I thought it was curious that sales were terrible until the sales force stopped being excited by the new product. Then, at the point where everybody was beginning to say, "This new machine isn't anything special," results took a dramatic turn for the better. I couldn't explain it because it seemed so much the opposite of common sense. You'd think that the machine would be most successful when it was new—with maximum sales-force enthusiasm and maximum competitive lead time. Now I know what was happening. As they became disillusioned, the attention of the salespeople turned away from the product and back to the customer.

There's a lesson here for anybody concerned with successful product launches. Several of our large multinational clients, on the basis of Huthwaite's research, now handle launches in a new way. Instead of giving Features and Advantages when they announce new products to the sales force, they concentrate on explaining the problems the product solves and on thinking up the questions that will uncover and develop these problems. It's proved a very successful method for speeding the growth curve of new-product sales.

Demonstrating Capability Effectively

What are the central messages in this chapter that will help you demonstrate your capability more effectively in larger sales? I would pick out three main practical points:

1. *Don't demonstrate capabilities too early in the call.* In smaller sales you can uncover a problem and jump straight in with Advantages about how you can solve it, but this doesn't work well in larger sales. It's important in larger sales to develop Explicit Needs—by using Implication and Need-payoff Questions—before you offer solutions. Presenting capabilities too soon is one of the most common mistakes in large accounts. It's made worse because many customers will encourage you to present solutions in the absence of any information about needs. "Just come and make a presentation about your product," they tell you, "and *we'll* decide whether it fits our needs." If you're forced to make presentations of Features and Advantages early in the selling cycle, always try to have a *minimum* of one premeeting with a key person in the account to uncover needs, so that your presentation includes at least some Benefits.

2. *Beware Advantages.* Most sales training, because it's based on models appropriate to smaller sales, encourages you to give Advantage statements when you sell. And to complicate the issue, the term they use for such statements is "Benefits." Don't let previous training mislead you. Remember that, in larger sales, the powerful statements are those which show that you can meet *Explicit Needs*. Don't fool yourself into thinking you're giving a lot of Benefits if you're not uncovering and meeting those Explicit Needs.

3. *Be careful with new products.* Most of us give far too many Features and Advantages when we're selling new products. Don't let this happen to you. Instead, the first thing to ask yourself about any new product is "What problems does it solve?" When you understand the problems it solves, you can plan SPIN questions to develop Explicit Needs. Try it. You'll be much more effective.

ANSWERS: Types of Product Statements

1. *Feature.* Balanced voltage stabilization is a fact about the system. The statement doesn't explain how stabilization can be used or can help the customer.

2. *Advantage.* This statement shows how the Feature in statement 1

can be used or can help the customer. It's not a Benefit because the customer hasn't expressed an Explicit Need for stabilization.

3. *Advantage.* The statement shows how backup memory can be used or can help the customer, so it's more than just a Feature. But because there's no evidence that the customer has expressed an Explicit Need for backup memory, we can't call it a Benefit.

4. *Feature.* Statements of cost (like this one) are facts or data about the product, so we classify them as Features.

5. *Benefit.* In the previous statement the customer has expressed an Explicit Need: "I need to be able to read source data straight into memory." In this statement the seller shows how the product meets that Explicit Need.

6. *Benefit.* Again, the buyer has stated an Explicit Need (an error rate less than 1 in 100,000). The seller shows that his product can easily meet the need.

7. *Advantage.* The seller shows another way in which having a low error rate can be used or can help the customer. However, as the next customer statement shows, this doesn't meet a need.

8. *Feature.* A piece of data about the product.

9. *Feature.* Further product facts.

10. *Advantage.* The seller shows how the Feature of time-based coding can be used to help the customer.

6
Preventing Objections

During a visit to the training center of a leading multinational company, I was invited to watch some sales training in progress. Instead of choosing the Advanced Systems Selling class, as my hosts had perhaps expected, I asked instead if I could sit in on a typical basic-skills program for new salespeople. Entering quietly at the back of the room, I looked around. The students all had that unnatural attentive cleanliness that goes with being new to sales. Their instructor, recently promoted from the field, was launching with great vigor into his favorite topic—objection handling. You couldn't have imagined a more typical scene. It could have been Day 2 of any basic sales-training program in any large corporation.

"The professional salesperson," the instructor began, "*welcomes* objections because they are a sign of customer interest. In fact, the more objections you get, the easier it will be for you to sell." The class, duly impressed, wrote this down. Meanwhile I groaned behind my mandatory visitor's smile. Here was yet another new generation of salespeople at the receiving end of one of the most misleading myths in selling. Still, as a visitor it would have been improper for me to comment, so I continued to smile through an hour of objection-handling techniques until the coffee break.

During the break, I talked with the instructor. "Did you believe what you were saying in there," I asked, "that stuff about the more objections, the easier to sell?"

"Yes," he replied. "If I didn't believe it, I wouldn't be teaching it."

I hesitated. Clearly the instructor and I had opposite views about objection handling. It would have been easier to drop the subject, but he'd

117

been kind enough to let me into his class, so I felt I owed him something in return. I asked, "You've been a successful sales performer for several years, haven't you?"

"Yes," he replied with some pride. "I've been with the company five years and I've made President's Club for the last three."

"Look back at your own sales experience," I urged him. "Five years ago, when you were new, did you receive more or fewer objections from your customers than you're getting now?"

He thought for a moment. "More, I guess." Then, as he remembered back, he added, "You know, in the two years when I was new, I seemed to get objections all the time."

"So in those first two years when you were facing all those objections, did you have good sales figures?"

"No," he said uncomfortably. "In fact, my sales weren't too good until my third year with the company."

Pressing the point, I asked him, "Then you did a lot better in that third year?"

"Yes, that was the year I first made President's Club."

"And how about objections? It sounds as if you had *more* objections in your unsuccessful years. How does that tie in with what you said in class about the more objections, the more successful the call will be?"

He considered the point for a while and said, "You're right. When I look back, I faced many more objections when I was unsuccessful. Perhaps I'm teaching the wrong message."

I had to admire him. Most people—given the astonishing human capacity for dismissing unwanted evidence—would have dodged the issue and held to their initial position. But the class was reconvening and I had to finish my tour of the facility, so I didn't have time to talk more with the instructor about objection handling. If we'd had more time, I would have told him:

- Objection handling is a much less important skill than most training makes it out to be.

- Objections, contrary to common belief, are more often created by the seller than the customer.

- In the average sales team, there's usually one salesperson who receives 10 times as many objections per selling hour as another person in the same team.

- Skilled people receive fewer objections because they have learned objection prevention, not objection handling.

To explain these findings, I'll have to go back to the discussion of Features, Advantages, and Benefits in Chapter 5. You'll remember the definitions of these three behaviors and their links to success in sales of different sizes (Figure 6.1). One of my colleagues, Linda Marsh, carried out some correlation studies to check whether there are statistically significant links between each of these behaviors and the most probable responses they produce from customers. For example, when sellers use a lot of Features in calls, do customers respond in a different way than in calls where *fewer* Features are used? She discovered that Features, Advantages, and Benefits each produce a different behavioral response from customers (Figure 6.2).

Features and Price Concerns

Customers are most likely to raise price concerns in calls where the seller gives lots of Features. Why is this? It seems that the effect of Features is to increase the customer's sensitivity to price. This isn't necessarily a bad thing if you happen to be selling low-cost products that are relatively rich in Features.

Consider the psychology of the advertisement shown in Figure 6.3. This features-rich product is being sold in a way that works well with cheaper goods. You can imagine a television commercial: "We give you

Behavior	Definition	Impact	
		On small sales	On larger sales
Features	Describe facts, data, product characteristics	Slightly positive	Neutral or slightly negative
Advantages (Type A Benefits)	Show how products, services, or their Features can be used or can help the customer	Positive	Slightly positive
Benefits (Type B Benefits)	Show how products or services meet Explicit Needs expressed by the customer	Very positive	Very positive

Figure 6.1. Features, Advantages, and Benefits.

Seller behavior	Most probable customer response
Features	Price concerns
Advantages	Objections
Benefits	Support or approval

Figure 6.2. Most probable effects of Features, Advantages, and Benefits on customers.

multiplication, division, subtraction...and what do you think that's worth? Well, don't answer yet because you also get mark-up and mark-down percentages—which is something you don't usually find on watches 10 times the price. And we also give you..." Throughout history, using Features this way has helped sell lower-priced goods. Why? Because Features increase price sensitivity. By listing all the Features, the customer comes to expect a higher price. When the product turns

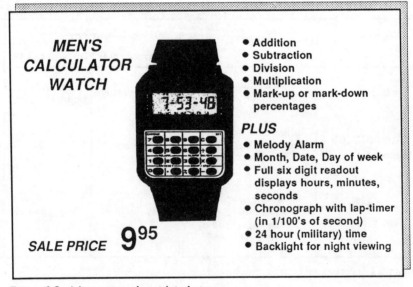

MEN'S CALCULATOR WATCH

- Addition
- Subtraction
- Division
- Multiplication
- Mark-up or mark-down percentages

PLUS

- Melody Alarm
- Month, Date, Day of week
- Full six digit readout displays hours, minutes, seconds
- Chronograph with lap-timer (in 1/100's of second)
- 24 hour (military) time
- Backlight for night viewing

SALE PRICE **9**⁹⁵

Figure 6.3. A low-cost product rich in features.

out to be much cheaper than its competition, the increased price sensitivity causes the buyer to feel extra positive about the lower price tag.

I chose a watch example, rather than an industrial product, because there's something unique about watches. In no other market that I can think of is there such an enormous price difference between competitors.

Now consider the advertisement shown in Figure 6.4. This watch is almost 100 times as expensive as the one in Figure 6.3. Do you think you'd be more likely to buy this expensive watch if there was a list of Features down the side of the advertisement to help persuade you? Not on your life! With top-of-the-market products, the price concern created by Features will make people *less* likely to buy. A list of Features would probably make you ask yourself questions about whether the expensive watch was worth it.

Too Many Features: A Case Study

The relationship between Features and price concerns isn't just a theoretical point that applies only to advertisers. It has clear implications for sales strategy. A major U.S.-based multinational corporation once called us in to help it with a problem. The corporation had been facing tough Japanese competition in its primary marketplace, particularly at the lower end of its product range. The Japanese products were richly featured and, as you might expect, somewhat less expensive than its own machines. As market share began to erode, the corporation looked for alternatives to price cutting. One attractive possibility was to introduce a new product with more Features that could compete directly with the Japanese machines. Such a machine would still be a little more expensive, but because of its added Features, it would provide a much stronger marketplace offering.

But who would sell this new product? The corporation decided to recruit part of the sales force from the competition. After all, nobody knew as much about how to sell these richly featured machines as the people who'd been successful sellers for the Japanese competitor. It seemed, on the face of it, a plausible strategy—recruiting experienced sellers while simultaneously weakening the competition by raiding its best people. The corporation's agents approached those salespeople who'd been very successful selling the cheaper Japanese machines and succeeded in recruiting some of the competitor's top people.

Unfortunately, these new people's sales results were deeply disappointing. The competition's superstars performed no better than the existing sales force. While trying to discover what was going wrong, I talked with several of the people recruited from the competition and

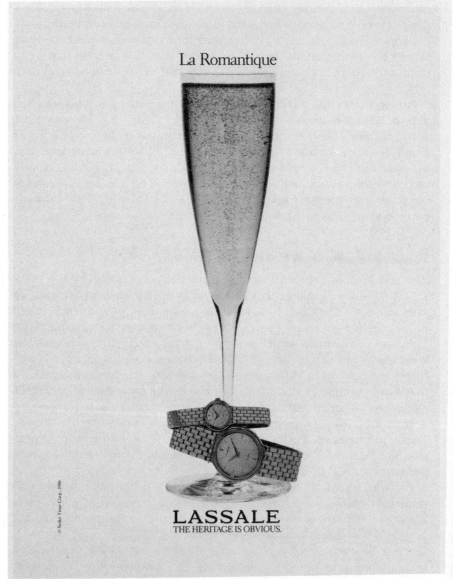

La Romantique

LASSALE
THE HERITAGE IS OBVIOUS.

Figure 6.4. A high-cost product. Listing features is a negative.

found them puzzled and dejected at their sudden fall from success. "It's price," they explained. "The product's too expensive; we get price objections all the time." And they were right. When we traveled with them on calls, we found that the number of price objections they received from customers was 30 percent higher than for the rest of the sales force who were selling the same product. Why? We couldn't write it off as pure coincidence when two sections of a sales force selling an identical product received different levels of price objections from their customers.

The answer lay in their use of Features. While selling for the cheaper competitor, these salespeople had developed a selling style very high in Features. This was very successful because, as we've seen, Features increase customers' price concerns. But because their product was cheaper, the price concern worked to their advantage. Now that they were selling for a more expensive competitor, the high level of Features they were giving worked against them. Their Features increased price concern and, because their product was more expensive, this turned customers toward the cheaper competitor. I presented our findings to the V.P. of Sales for the division. As he wryly remarked, "Right now, they seem to be doing a better job of selling for our competition than when our competition employed them." How could we help? Not, I suggested, by teaching them how to handle price objections. That was just a symptom. It would be more effective to treat the *cause* and help these new people adopt a selling style more appropriate to a top-of-the-market product. So we retrained them in SPIN questioning techniques so that they could use a high-Benefits style. As a result, their sales increased, price objections dropped, and the price issues were soon forgotten.

Treating Symptoms or Treating Causes?

Let me introduce a theme that I'll come back to several times in this chapter. Curing a selling problem, just like curing a disease, rests on finding and treating the *cause* rather than the symptoms.

When I was 9 years old I lived in Borneo. A friend of my own age warned me that there was a typhoid epidemic in the village. All that either of us knew about typhoid was that it caused a burning fever. "But I won't catch it," he assured me; "I'm eating a lot of ice cream to keep cool." I followed his example—and caught typhoid from infected ice cream. One of the few things I remember clearly about my month seriously ill in the hospital was my father explaining to me the differences between symptoms, such as a high temperature, and causes, such as the nasty little bacterium *Salmonella typhosa* that loves to lurk in ice cream.

Perhaps this episode made me unduly sensitive to treating symptoms when you should be watching out for causes. But just suppose we'd run a program to teach those salespeople clever answers to price objections.

Would we have achieved anything? I think not. The customer's price concern was just a symptom. The cause was giving too many Features. Teaching objection-handling skills would do no more to prevent price concerns than eating ice cream would prevent typhoid.

Advantages and Objections

Perhaps the most fascinating of the links that Linda Marsh found is the strong relationship between Advantages and objections. You'll remember that Advantages are statements that show how products or their Features can be used or can help the customer—statements that many of us have been trained to call "Benefits." Chapter 5 showed that Advantages have a positive effect on small sales but a much less positive effect when the sale grows larger, and Linda's discovery offers a partial explanation of this. Advantages create objections—and this is one reason why they are poorly linked to success in the large sale.

To help understand the link between Advantages and objections, consider the following extract from an actual sales call. I've edited out references to the company and I've cut the length of some statements; otherwise, this exact sequence of behaviors happened in a call we recorded in Dallas in September 1981. The product being sold is a word processor.

> SELLER: *(Problem Question)* Does all this retyping waste time?
>
> BUYER: *(Implied Need)* Yeah, some. But there's not so much of it here, not like in Fort Worth.
>
> SELLER: *(Advantage)* Here's where our word processors would be a real big help because they'd eliminate that retyping for you.
>
> BUYER: *(objection)* Look, we retype stuff, sure. But you won't get me paying for fancy $15,000 machines just to cut down on some retyping.
>
> SELLER: *(Advantage)* I understand you, but the labor costs of retyping can climb out of sight. A big plus of word processors is that they save you money by making your people more efficient.
>
> BUYER: *(objection)* We're very efficient right now—and if I wanted to do better on efficiency I can think of 16 ways without new word processors. I've two xxx word processors there in the back office. Nobody much knows how to use them. They give trouble, just trouble.
>
> SELLER: *(Problem Question)* Those xxx machines are hard for your people to use?
>
> BUYER: *(Implied Need)* Yes, it's quicker to type it out by hand—doing it the old way.
>
> SELLER: *(Advantage)* We really can help you there. Our yyy machines use a screen, so people can see exactly what they're doing. That's a lot better than your old xxx's where you've got to remember things like format

codes—which we prompt automatically, so that our machine can be used much more easily.

BUYER: *(objection)* Know what? Some of the ladies working here get uptight about a typewriter with a correcting ribbon. Screen? It'd just confuse the hell out of them. I'd end up with more mistakes than I'm getting now.

SELLER: *(Problem Question)* You're getting too many mistakes?

BUYER: *(Implied Need)* Some. Well, no more than most offices, but more than I like.

SELLER: *(Advantage)* Tests show that with the full-screen editing and error correction we offer, your error rates would drop by more than 20 percent if you used our machines.

BUYER: *(objection)* Yeah, but it's not worth all that hassle just to get rid of a few typos.

What's happened here? The first thing you'll notice is that every Advantage is followed by an objection. Of course, I've chosen this extract to illustrate my point, for objections don't *always* follow Advantages the way they do in the example I've picked here. Sometimes the seller will use an Advantage that brings a favorable response from the customer. But from our research, objections are a more likely response than any other buyer behavior (Figure 6.5).

The next thing to notice about this example is the characteristic sequence of behaviors: Problem QuestionlImplied Needlobjection. We found this sequence happening over and over again in unsuccessful calls. Let's look more closely at what's going on.

As you can see, the fundamental problem that's causing the objection is that the seller offered a solution before building up the need. The buyer doesn't feel that the problem has enough *value* to merit such an expensive solution. Consequently, when the seller gives the Advantage, the buyer raises an objection.

This explains why Advantages have a more positive effect in small sales. If the word processor had cost $15 instead of $15,000, the buyer would probably have reacted differently. It's certainly worth $15 to eliminate retyping. But $15,000? That's a different matter.

Back to Symptoms and Causes

How would you help the seller in our example? It's tempting to suggest that because she is receiving so many objections, what she needs is better objection-handling skills. So, for example, we could teach her *principles* of objection handling—the classic techniques of acknowledging, rephrasing, and answering. Or we could give her *specific* help with the

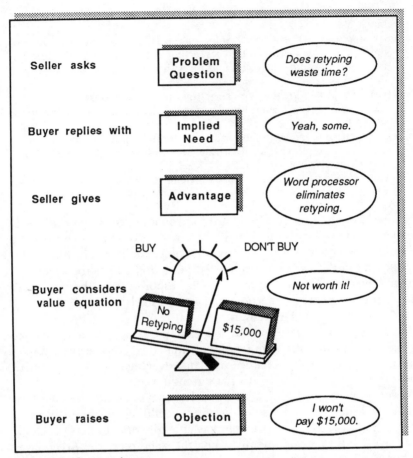

Figure 6.5. Creating objections.

common objections that customers raise by showing her what to say when customers raise such typical objections as:

Your word processors are too expensive.

Word processors are hard to use.

My people would be resistant to word processors.

Word processors are more hassle than they're worth.

Either of these options would help her handle future objections better. But are we treating the symptom or the cause? In each case in the example, the objection arose because the seller hadn't built sufficient *value* before offering solutions. Teaching her how to handle objections treats the symptom, but it doesn't alter the cause. The fundamental selling disease—jumping in too soon with solutions—remains malignant and untreated.

The Cure

If objection handling just treats a symptom, how would we set about a complete cure? This is where the SPIN Model comes in. By teaching her to probe in a way that builds *value*, we can prevent the objection from arising in the first place. Let me show you what I mean, using the final objection in the example. First let's examine why the customer raised the objection in the first place.

> SELLER: *(Problem Question)* You're getting too many mistakes?
> BUYER: *(Implied Need)* Some. Well, no more than most offices, but more than I like.
> SELLER: *(Advantage)* Tests show that with the full-screen editing and error correction we offer, your error rates would drop by more than 20 percent if you used our machines.
> BUYER: *(objection)* Yeah, but it's not worth all that hassle just to get rid of a few typos.

The customer has raised the objection because he doesn't perceive sufficient *value* from reducing the error rate. If you could draw a value-equation diagram to show what was going on in the customer's mind, it would probably look like the one in Figure 6.6. The hassle greatly outweighs the value of eliminating a few mistakes, so the customer makes a negative judgment and raises an objection. Even the best objection-handling skills can't alter the fact that the seller has offered a solution without first building value.

Let's look at how a more skilled person would handle the same situation:

> SELLER: *(Problem Question)* You're getting too many mistakes?
> BUYER: *(Implied Need)* Some. Well, no more than most offices, but more than I like.
> SELLER: *(Implication Question)* You say "more than you'd like. Does this mean that some of those mistakes are causing you difficulties in documents you send out to clients?
> BUYER: Sometimes that's happened, but not often, because I proofread all important documents carefully before I send them out.
> SELLER: *(Implication Question)* Doesn't that take up a lot of your time?
> BUYER: Too much. But it's better than letting a document go out with a mistake—particularly if it's a mistake in the figures that go out to a client.

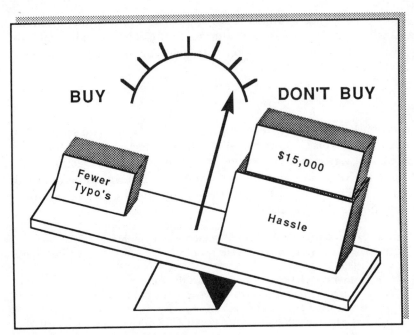

Figure 6.6. How the customer sees it.

SELLER: *(Implication Question)* Why would that be? Are you saying that a mistake in the figures would lead to more serious consequences with clients than a mistake in the text would?

BUYER: Oh yes. We could lose a bid, or commit ourselves to an uneconomic contract—or even just come across to clients as sloppy. People judge you on things like that. That's why it's worth a couple of hours a day proofreading when there's other things I should be doing.

SELLER: *(Need-payoff Question)* Suppose you didn't have to spend that time proofreading. What could you do with the time you saved?

BUYER: Well, I could give some time to training my office people.

SELLER: *(Need-payoff Question)* And this training would lead to improved productivity?

BUYER: Oh, very much. At the moment, you see, people don't know how to use some of the equipment here—that graph plotter for example—so they have to wait until I'm free to do it.

SELLER: *(Implication Question)* So the time you're spending in proofing also forces you to become a bottleneck for other people's work?

BUYER: Yes. I'm badly overloaded.

SELLER: *(Need-payoff Question)* Then anything that reduced the time you're spending in proofing wouldn't just help you, it would also help the productivity of others?

BUYER: Right.

SELLER: *(Need-payoff Question)* I can see how by reducing proofreading you could ease the present bottleneck. Is there any other way that having fewer mistakes in documents would help you?

BUYER: Sure. People here hate retyping. It might be a plus in terms of their motivation if fewer mistakes meant less time spent in retyping.

SELLER: *(Need-payoff Question)* And presumably less time in retyping would also bring cost savings?

BUYER: You're right. And that's something I need to do.

SELLER: *(summarizing)* So it seems that the present level of mistakes is leading to expensive retyping, which creates a motivation problem with your people. If mistakes, particularly in figures, get out to your clients, it can be very damaging. You're trying to prevent that at the moment by spending 2 hours a day proofing all key documents. But that's turning you into a bottleneck, reducing everyone's productivity and preventing you from putting time into training your staff.

BUYER: When you put it that way, those mistakes in documents are really hurting us. We can't just ignore the problem—I've got to do something about it.

SELLER: *(Benefit)* Then let me show you how our word processor would help you cut mistakes and reduce proofing...

If we were to reexamine the customer's value equation now, it would probably look like the one in Figure 6.7.

Now the cost and hassle are more than counterbalanced by the *value* the seller has created through the use of Implication and Need-payoff Questions. It's a much more effective piece of selling because we've attacked the *cause* of the objection. As a result, the objection doesn't even arise. Objection prevention turns out to be a superior strategy to objection handling.

Objection Prevention: A Case Study

I can imagine people reading this and saying to themselves, "Yes, it all sounds very plausible when Rackham's making up examples that suit his case, but I'm not sure it holds up in the real world." As a further piece of evidence, then, I'd like to share with you one of the most fascinating little investigations I was ever involved with.

The company was a well-known high-tech corporation whose personnel research staff had been investigating sales behavior in one of its divisions based in the southern United States. We had encouraged the research staff to use the behavior-analysis method of counting how often key seller and customer behaviors occurred during sales calls, and they had come up with a curious finding. The average sales team in the division consisted of eight salespeople. Now purely in terms of statistical

Figure 6.7. The customer develops a new point of view.

probabilities, you'd expect that these eight people, each selling the same product to the same size of customer and with the same competitors, would each face approximately the same number of objections per selling hour. Not so. There was an enormous difference in the number of objections faced by individual salespeople. In the average team they often found one salesperson having to face *10 times* as many objections per selling hour as other people from the same team.

The research staff didn't know about our work on the links between Advantages and objections. Naturally, they drew the obvious conclusion: The people who were receiving so many objections must need training in objection handling. They asked us for advice. One quick look at their data told us what we needed to know. We picked the behavior-analysis figures for 10 people who were each receiving very high numbers of objections and who were clearly candidates for objection-handling training. In all 10 cases, these people were higher than average in the number of Advantages they used in their calls.

I persuaded the company to try a bold experiment. "What I'd like to do," I explained, "is to train these people in objection *prevention*. I think we can design a program which doesn't even mention the word *objection* but which will do more for these people than the best objection-handling training ever could." The company agreed. We chose eight salespeople who—from the behavior-analysis figures—had each received an unusually high level of objections from customers. As we'd promised, our training didn't say anything at all about objections or objection handling. Instead, we taught the eight people to develop Explicit Needs with the SPIN Model and then to offer Benefits.

After the training, the company's researchers went out with the eight to count the number of objections they were now receiving in calls. The average number of objections per selling hour had fallen by 55 percent. I'd draw two conclusions from this little study:

- It confirms that the best way to handle objections is through prevention. Treat the cause, not the symptom.

- Notice that our training didn't prevent objections *completely*.

There will always be objections that arise because the customer has needs your product can't meet or because a competitor has a clear product superiority. These "true" objections are facts of life, and no objection-prevention technique can do anything to stop them from being raised. However, what we were able to show in this case was that objections can be cut by more than half by using the SPIN behaviors to build value.

The Sales-Training Approach to Objections

Traditional sales training actually teaches people to *create* objections, then teaches them techniques for handling the objections they've inadvertently created. This is because the selling-skills models in every major sales-training program we've reviewed have been based on the small sale. As we've seen, in small sales a high level of Advantages can be successful because there's less need to build value before offering solutions—but in larger sales Advantages don't have this positive impact. (It's important to remember that we're using the term *Advantage* to cover any statement that shows how your product or service can be used or can help the customer; in other words, what we're calling an Advantage is what most sales training calls a Benefit.)

It's my hope, as training designers begin to understand that larger sales need different skills, that we'll see an end to the kind of training that encourages salespeople to give a lot of Advantages. The heavy use of Advantages—which is what most training recommends—is the cause of more than half of the objections that customers raise. But are objections necessarily bad? Some sales-training programs and many sales trainers, such as the instructor I described at the first of this chapter, teach that objections are positively linked to success and that the more you get, the better. If that's true, then preventing objections could actually *hurt* your selling. What does the evidence tell us?

We carried out a study to find out whether objections were really "sales opportunities in disguise," as one training program put it. We counted the number of objections raised by customers in a sample of 694 calls collected from an international sample in a large business-machines corporation. Figure 6.8 shows the results.

As you can see, the higher the percentage of objections in the customer's behavior, the less likely that the call will succeed. If objections are

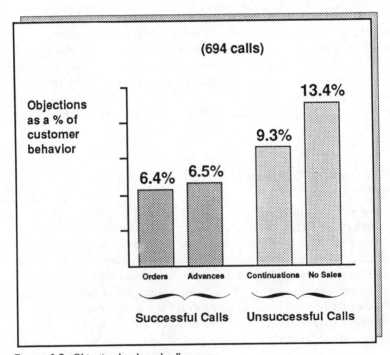

Figure 6.8. Objection levels and call success.

sales opportunities in disguise, then this study suggests that their disguise must have been created by a master in camouflage. No, make no mistake about it, the more objections you get in a call, the less likely you are to be successful. It's a comforting myth for trainers to tell inexperienced salespeople that professionals welcome objections as a sign of customer interest, but in reality an objection is a barrier between you and your customer. However skillfully you dismantle this barrier through objection handling, it would be smarter not to have created it in the first place.

Benefits and Support/Approval

The most positive relationship to emerge from Linda Marsh's study of Features, Advantages, and Benefits is the strong link between giving Benefits and receiving expressions of approval or support from customers. She found that the more Benefits the sellers gave, the more approving statements their customers made. This isn't a surprising finding. After all, Benefits—as we define them—involve showing how you can meet an Explicit Need that the customer has expressed. Unless the customer first says, "I want it," you can't give a Benefit. It's no wonder that customers are most likely to express approval when you show you can give them something they want.

Objection Handling versus Objection Prevention

At its most basic, what I've suggested in this chapter is that the old objection-*handling* strategies, which encourage the seller to give Advantages, are much less successful in the larger sale than objection-*prevention* strategies, where the seller first develops value using Implication and Need-payoff Questions before offering capabilities (Figure 6.9).

When I was new to selling I thought that, next to closing, objection-handling skills were the ones most crucial to sales success. Looking back, I can now see that my concern was motivated by the large number of objections I was facing from my customers. I didn't ask myself what caused the objections—but just knew that there were lots of them, so I'd better improve my objection handling. I now understand that the majority of objections I faced were only a symptom caused by poor selling. By improving my probing skills, I've become more successful at objection prevention—and this has certainly helped me sell more success-

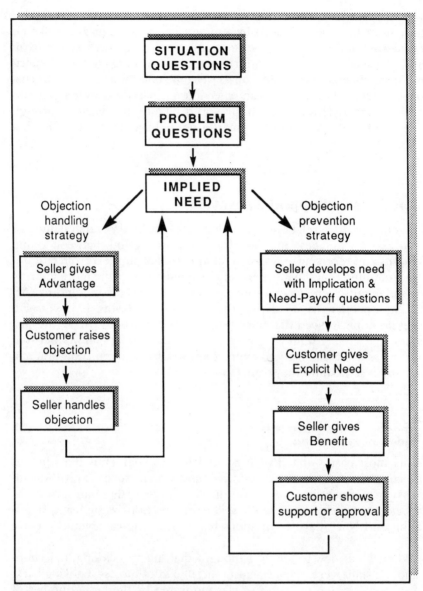

Figure 6.9. Objection handling or objection prevention?

fully. I still get objections, of course, for in selling there will always be the potential for a genuine mismatch between customer needs and what a seller can offer. So objection-handling skills will always have a part to play in my calls. But the reason I sell better now isn't better objection-handling skills, it's that I'm less likely to create unnecessary objections.

Preventing Objections from Your Customers

If you're receiving more objections from customers than you'd like, think about which is symptom and which is cause. Could it be that objections are just a symptom you've caused by offering your solutions too soon in the call? Try putting extra effort into effective needs development, using Implication and Need-payoff Questions. If you can build the *value* of your solutions, then you're much less likely to face objections. As many hundreds of salespeople we've trained will testify, good questioning skills will do more to help you with objections than any objection-handling techniques ever could.

Of course, you'll always get *some* objections, especially when your product doesn't meet a customer's needs. However, here are two sure signs that you're getting *unnecessary* objections that can be prevented by better questioning:

1. *Objections early in the call.* Customers rarely object to questions—unless you've found a particularly offensive way to ask them. Most objections are to solutions that don't fit needs. If you're getting a lot of objections early in the call, it probably means that instead of asking questions, you've been prematurely offering solutions and capabilities. The cure is simple enough: Don't talk about solutions until you've asked enough questions to develop strong needs.

2. *Objections about value.* If most of the objections you receive raise doubts about the *value* of what you offer, then there's a good chance that you're not developing needs strongly enough. Typical value objections would be "It's too expensive," "I don't think it's worth the trouble of changing from our existing supplier," or "We're happy with our existing system." In cases like these, customer objections tell you that you haven't succeeded in building a strong need. The solution lies in better needs development, not in objection handling. Particularly if you're getting a lot of price objections, cut down on the use of Features and, instead, concentrate on asking Problem, Implication, and Need-payoff Questions.

7

Preliminaries:
Opening the Call

In this chapter I want to examine Preliminaries more closely. To be honest, the Huthwaite research team didn't find the Preliminaries stage of the call very exciting when compared with the central areas of Investigating and Demonstrating Capability. Perhaps this is our personal bias. At any rate, it meant that we did much less research about this stage than about the other three (Figure 7.1). Nevertheless, even the limited data we did collect showed that successful ways of opening the call in a small sale are different from those which work best as the size of the sale increases.

How important is the warming-up stage of the call? In our research on Preliminaries we sought the answers to a number of questions, including these:

- Is it true that the first impressions made in a sales call are crucial to its success?

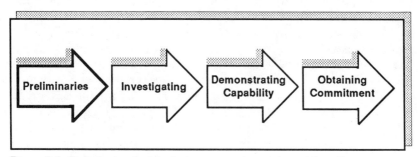

Figure 7.1. Preliminaries: the introductory or warming-up stage of the call.

- Do the openings that work in smaller sales work equally well in larger ones?

- Does one particular way work better than others to open a call?

Before examining these questions, I should note that in discussing Preliminaries in the larger sale, this chapter simplifies the situation by talking mainly about first meetings with new customers. As we know, of course, most larger sales involve several calls and are likely to be with customers with whom we already have an established relationship; with some major-account groups I've known, less than 5 percent of their calls were first-time meetings with new customers. However, the factors that influence Preliminaries in the multi-call sale have not, to my knowledge, been researched by anyone. It seems likely that as the selling cycle progresses, whether with old or new customers, the impact of Preliminaries diminishes because the relationship has become well established. But nobody knows for sure, and I'd prefer to avoid speculation.

Consequently, I'm going to concentrate on areas where some data exists. Although we don't have research about the impact of Preliminaries across a whole sales cycle, we *do* have information about opening first calls on new customers in both large and small sales.

First Impressions

There's evidence to suggest that people notice far less in the early stages of an interaction than we may imagine. Many of the older books on selling emphasize the importance of a smart appearance and suggest that first impressions will make or break the sale, but most of the recent research suggests that initial appearances are far less important than these older writers have claimed. This is not to say that it pays to be scruffy or unpresentable. A reasonable standard of dress is probably sensible. But don't believe that tiny details will make a big difference to your sales success in the Preliminaries stage of the sale. As we've seen, the far more important and more durable impressions are made during the Investigating stage.

In the early stages of an interaction with another person, we're usually so overloaded with information that we either don't notice, or we quickly forget, some quite obvious things. How often have you been introduced to someone and, 10 seconds later, forgotten his or her name? Why should you forget something as important as a name? Because your mind is full of other things, such as what you're going to say next. You literally don't have room for all the details available to you. Many potentially important impressions get crowded out in the opening minutes of a meeting.

It's hard to get accurate data on the importance of first impressions, so let me give you my personal opinion from having watched the openings of many hundreds of sales calls. Over and over again I've seen successful calls that started in a nondescript or even awkward manner, and I've seen tremendously smooth openings lead nowhere. Over the years I've come to doubt the importance of first impressions during the Preliminary stage of the call. I no longer believe that first impressions can make or break your sales success in larger sales.

Now it may be that such things as dress or opening words do matter in very small sales. A friend of mine was raising money for a charity by door-to-door selling of Christmas cards. I believe him when he claims that there was a direct relationship between how his volunteers dressed and how much they sold. One day, he told me, he insisted that they all wear their best clothes. Sales went up by 20 percent. But don't expect a smart suit and a good opening sentence to add 20 percent to your sales volume if you're in major-account selling.

Conventional Openings

Since the 1920s, salespeople have been taught that there are two successful ways to open a call:

- *Relate to the buyer's personal interests.* The conventional sales wisdom says that if you can somehow tap into an area of personal interest, then you can form a relationship more quickly and the call will be more successful. For example, if your buyer has a photograph of children on the desk, discuss family interests; if there's a golf trophy in the office, talk golf.

- *Make an opening benefit statement.* Begin with some dramatic statement about the benefits your product can offer. For example, you might say, "Ms. Customer, in today's marketplace productivity is the central concern of key executives like yourself—and our product will contribute to *your* productivity."

Our evidence suggests that, while these two methods might be successful in smaller sales, there's little to show that they help you when the sale is larger. Let's review this evidence.

Relating to Personal Interests

In one of Huthwaite's early studies, carried out in part of the Imperial Group, we were trying to establish whether salespeople who built good relationships would, as a result, make more sales. We found that sellers

who dealt successfully with small retail outlets in rural areas seemed to
rely heavily on personal factors in their selling. We measured the number of times each seller referred to some fact or incident related to the
customer's personal life. For example, the seller might ask, "How's Ann
enjoying her riding lessons?" or "Is Joe's leg better yet?" In rural areas,
where the size of sale was small, successful sellers used more of these
personal references than did sellers who were less successful. So we
could safely conclude that the old advice is right: If you can relate to
points of personal interest, it will help your selling.

But it was a different story in the large urban stores, where the average sale was more than 5 times the size. We found no relationship between success and reference to personal issues. Therefore, it seemed
that relating to the buyer's personal interests might be a less effective
technique in larger sales. But I wasn't particularly satisfied with this
study; for a number of technical reasons, we had to be cautious about
our interpretation. For example, the rural salespeople generally had
longer tenure and a lower turnover rate. This meant that they had been
on the job longer and had thus had more opportunity to find out personal things about their customers. And the rural customers themselves
were less busy than their large urban counterparts, so they had more
time to talk.

Nevertheless, this study raised some questions. It was possibly true in
the 1920s, when the theory was first put forward, that people bought
from those they related to personally; friends did business with friends.
But even in the mere 15 years I've been studying selling, I've noticed a
distinct change. Fifteen years ago buyers would tell me, "I buy from
Fred because I like him." Now I'm much more likely to hear, "I like
Fred, but I buy from his competition because they're cheaper." It seems
that personal loyalty is no longer an adequate basis for doing business.

There's another reason why it may not be successful to open the call
around a personal point. I once worked with the central purchasing
group of British Petroleum. On the wall of his office, one of the buyers
had a picture of a racing yacht. "I keep it there because it improves my
efficiency," he told me. Puzzled, I asked him to explain. "I get salespeople coming in here every day," he said, "wasting my time by talking
about a lot of nonbusiness issues. Obviously they're fishing for some
personal area that will catch my interest. But I'm a busy professional
purchaser—and I couldn't get through the day if I wasted time on conversation that isn't directly business-related. So I use the picture to increase my productivity. When new sales reps visit me for the first time,
they usually say, 'What a beautiful picture. You must really enjoy sailing.' I reply, 'I *hate* sailing. That picture's there to remind me how
much time gets wasted out on the water. Now what did you want to see
me about?'"

Perhaps that's an extreme case, but I've heard many other professional buyers complain about salespeople who try to open calls by cultivating areas of personal interest. The last thing a busy buyer wants is to tell the tenth seller of the day all about his last game of golf. The more senior the people you're selling to, the more they feel their time is at a premium, and the more impatience you're likely to generate if you dwell on nonbusiness areas. And there's another reason. Many buyers become suspicious of people who begin by raising areas of personal interest. They feel that the seller's motives aren't genuine and that it's an attempt to manipulate them.

I'm not saying that you should never begin a sales call by talking about a buyer's personal interests. Sometimes, particularly if the buyer takes the lead in raising an area, it's the right thing to do. And as we've seen, in smaller sales there can be an overall positive impact on sales success from raising personal issues. But as a general piece of advice, I suggest that you be careful not to overuse this method in larger sales.

The Opening Benefit Statement

Many sales-training programs teach that the most effective way to begin the call is to make an opening benefit statement to catch the buyer's interest with some potential benefit of your product or service. So I might say, "Mr. Wilson, for a busy executive like yourself, I know that time is money. And I'm sure you waste a lot of time looking up telephone numbers and dialing calls. With the Rackham Autodialer I could help save some of that time for you." If it's well done, an opening benefit statement can sound positive and businesslike. But is it an effective way to open calls?

Although the idea of the opening benefit statement is quite old—I've been able to trace it back 30 years and it might even go back further than that—its great popularity as an opening was brought about by the Xerox Learning Systems program, Professional Selling Skills (PSS). This program was very widely used, and its developers claimed that research showed that calls were more likely to be successful if they started this way—using, as they called it, an Initial Benefit Statement. I haven't seen the detailed research, so I can't comment on its validity. But I do know that the investigation on which the program was based took place in the pharmaceutical industry—where the average call length was a mere 6 minutes. If you've only 6 minutes of buyer time, then I could certainly see why you would need a punchy way to get straight into the substance of your call.

But would the same be true in larger sales, where the average individual call length is 40 minutes? Huthwaite set out to investigate this. We watched just over 300 calls, noting whether or not the seller used an opening benefit statement. Then, using the procedure described in Chapter 1, we divided the calls into those which succeeded and those which failed. If opening benefit statements made calls more successful, as the PSS program claimed, then we should expect to find that the calls which failed had fewer opening benefit statements than those which succeeded. This is not what we found. In our studies there was no relationship, one way or another, between the use of opening benefit statements and the success of the call.

Why should this useful-sounding method, the opening benefit statement, not be related to success in some way? We decided to look more closely.

What we found was this. The most effective salespeople we studied opened each call in a different way. Sometimes they might use an opening benefit statement, but frequently they would use some other starting point. Less effective people were the ones who tended to open each call in the same way. So those sellers who began *every* call with an opening benefit statement were likely to be less successful than those who just used the technique occasionally.

Larger sales mean multiple calls—often several on the same customer—so it's particularly important not to use a standard opening more than once with the same person. I can recall how impressed I was with a salesperson from an office products company when he first called on me. He began with a classic opening benefit statement: "Mr. Rackham, you're a busy executive and I'm sure you're wondering whether it's worth 15 minutes of your time to talk with me. But if, as a result of that 15 minutes, you could save your company several thousand dollars, I'm sure you'd agree that it would be time well spent." So I gave him 15 minutes and was sufficiently impressed with his product to invite him back the following week to talk to us again. At the next meeting, with my office manager present, he began, "Mr. Rackham, I know you're busy, but if I could use 15 minutes of your time to show you how I could save your company thousands of dollars,..." The very opening that had made such a positive impression the first time around now sounded mechanical and irritating.

There's another reason why the opening benefit statement may be ineffective. Successful salespeople talk about their products or services late in the sales call, but we've seen that less successful people begin talking products and solutions very much earlier in the call. I remind you of this point here because it raises one of the dangers of using opening benefit statements. Take this simple example:

SELLER: *(using opening benefit statement)* Mr. Buzzard, we at Big Co know how important it is to produce professional-looking documents in a business like yours. That's why we invented the Executype typewriter. Using a special new system, the Executype gives a far finer finish to your documents than you can get from conventional word processors.

BUYER: *(asking the questions)* Oh. Does it use a daisy wheel?

SELLER: *(drawn into giving product details)* No, it's an ink-jet process.

BUYER: *(still asking the questions)* Ink jet? That must be very expensive, Ms. Simpson. What does it cost?

SELLER: *(forced into a price issue early in the call)* Er...well, it *is* a little more expensive than conventional methods, but it's also got...

What's happened here? By making an opening benefit statement, the seller has been trapped in two ways:

- She's been forced to talk about product details too early in the sale, before she's had an opportunity to build value by using SPIN questions.

- She's allowed the *buyer* to ask the questions and has therefore allowed him to take control of the discussion.

Neither of these traps is irreversible. If she's smart, Ms. Simpson will recover the call, take over the questioning role from the buyer, and turn attention away from the product and back toward the customer's needs. But at the very least, this isn't a good way to begin the sale. Yet I've personally seen many calls start this way because the seller used an opening benefit statement.

A Framework for Opening the Call

So far, much of this chapter has been negative—how *not* to handle the Preliminaries stage of the call. Let's turn our attention to the positives. What does Huthwaite's research recommend as the best way to open calls? Obviously, as I've suggested, variety is important. There isn't one best opening technique. But there *is* a framework that successful people use.

Focusing on Your Objective

Let's examine the objective of the Preliminaries stage of a call. What's the purpose of your opening? At its very simplest, what you're trying to do is to get the customer's consent to move on to the next phase—the Investigating stage. You want customers to agree that it's legitimate for you to ask them some questions. In order to do this, you must establish:

- Who you are
- Why you're there (but not by giving product details)
- Your right to ask questions

Obviously there are many ways to open the call, but the common factor of most good openings is that they lead the customer to agree that *you* should ask questions. In doing so, good openings keep you from getting into detailed discussions of products or services. Early in the call you want to establish your role as the seeker of information and the buyer's role as the giver.

Making Your Preliminaries Effective

Preliminaries, as we've seen, don't play a crucial role in the larger sale. The most important test of whether you're handling Preliminaries effectively is whether your customers are generally happy to move ahead and answer your questions. If so, then you're probably handling this stage of the call acceptably. Don't worry about appearing smooth and polished—some of the best salespeople we've studied have seemed nervous, self-conscious, or hesitant in the early minutes of the call. But do be concerned about these three points:

1. *Get down to business quickly.* Don't dawdle. The Preliminaries stage is not the most productive part of the call for you or for the customer. A common mistake, particularly for inexperienced salespeople, is spending too long on pleasantries. As a result, the call runs short of time—the customer has to stop just when you're getting to a critical point. If you find that your calls often run out of time, it's worth asking yourself whether you're getting down to business quickly enough. While there's no exact measure for how long it should take to open a call, I'd be worried by anyone who consistently spent more than 20 percent of the call time on Preliminaries.

Don't feel that you'll offend customers by getting down to business quickly. A complaint I frequently hear from senior executives and professional buyers is that salespeople waste their time with idle chatter. I don't think I've ever heard the complaint that a salesperson gets down to business too quickly.

2. *Don't talk about solutions too soon.* One of the most common faults in selling is talking about your solutions and capabilities too early in the call. As we've seen in previous chapters, offering solutions too soon causes objections and greatly reduces the chances that the call will succeed. How often do you find yourself discussing your products, ser-

vices, or solutions with the customer during the first half of the call? If it happens frequently, then it may be a sign that you're not handling the Preliminaries effectively.

If, in your case, it's usually the customer who is asking the questions and you're in the role of providing facts and explanations, then it's likely that you've not sufficiently established your role as a questioner during the Preliminaries. Ask yourself whether your call opening establishes that *you* should be asking the questions. If it doesn't establish this, change the way you open calls so that the customer accepts that you'll be asking some questions before you talk about the capabilities you can offer.

3. *Concentrate on questions.* Never forget that the Preliminaries aren't the most important part of the call. Often, when I've been traveling with salespeople, I've noticed that they waste time before a call worrying about how they should open it when they could be using that time far more effectively to plan some questions instead.

8

Turning Theory into Practice

One of my favorite words, *entelechy,* is so little known that listeners reach for a dictionary whenever I use it. That's a pity, because the word fills a serious gap in the English language and deserves to be in every-day circulation. It means the becoming actual of what was potential—turning something into practical usefulness as opposed to theoretical elegance. Entelechy is the subject of this chapter—turning the potentials of Huthwaite's research into actions that will be practically useful to you in your selling.

There's no easy way to convert theoretical models into practical skills. The fact that you're reading this book doesn't mean that the knowledge you're gaining will automatically translate itself into improved selling abilities. No book on selling will, of itself, improve your selling skills, any more than reading a book about swimming will teach you how to swim. The challenge for both author and reader in any book with pretensions to being practical is entelechy—turning theory into practical action.

To meet my part of the challenge, I'll draw on Huthwaite's worldwide experience of training many thousands of people to improve their selling skills. In this chapter I'll share with you some of the principles and practices that have worked successfully for us and for our clients. Your challenge is a tougher one, because improving your skills is hard work; there's no instant formula for better selling. Success in any skill—whether in golf, playing the piano, or selling—rests on concentrated, tedious, and frustrating practice. It's quite realistic for you to expect a significant increase in your sales results if you follow the advice in this book and *really practice* the skills, but this is the tough bit. For each reader who practices adequately, a dozen are likely to fall by the way-side.

The Four Golden Rules for Learning Skills

Why do people find it so difficult to learn skills? It's not just because of the hard work, for we're accustomed to putting work into learning new knowledge. You've demonstrated the ability to work hard already, through the time and energy you've invested in reading this book—in acquiring *knowledge* about how to sell. Yet I wonder how many readers will invest an equivalent amount of effort in turning their knowledge into practice. The sad fact is that we generally work harder and more effectively to learn knowledge than to translate our knowledge into skills. Perhaps *entelechy* is such a rare word because it refers to some-thing we so rarely do.

It's my personal belief that the main reason why people have such trouble improving their skills is that they've never thought about the ba-sic techniques of skill learning. At school our success depended on de-veloping techniques for learning knowledge—and most of us got quite good at it. But what did school do to help us learn skills systematically? With the exception of sports, the answer for most people is little or nothing. So before I talk about *what* skills you should practice, it will be useful to begin with *how*. How can you learn *any* skill efficiently and with minimum pain?

We have found that most people can greatly improve their ability to learn skills if they stick by four simple rules.

Rule 1: Practice Only One Behavior at a Time

Most people, when they work on improving their skills, try to do too much at once. I can imagine people reading this book and saying, "I'm going to cut out closing techniques, and in future I'll ask more Problem Questions. Then, instead of jumping in with solutions—which is what I usually do—I'll hold back and ask Implication Questions...oh, and Need-payoff Questions too, of course. And I'll also work on avoiding Features and Advantages; instead, I'll make more Benefits and..." *STOP!* If that's how you're thinking, then in terms of learning, you're dead. People who successfully learn complex skills do so by practicing one behavior at a time—not by half-practicing two, and certainly not by trying to handle 10 at once.

Last year I was on a flight to Australia and found myself sitting opposite a delightful man named Tom Landry. As an Englishman, my sports are cricket and croquet—I knew nothing of American football. Consequently, it wasn't until well into the conversation that it emerged that Mr. Landry was a famous football coach. I confess, right up to that moment, I'd mistakenly thought the Dallas Cowboys were a traveling rodeo show. So I was fascinated when Tom Landry explained a little about the sophisticated and complex task of coaching a major football team.

"Your job is teaching people skills," I prompted him. "If you had to put forward just one principle for successfully learning a skill, what would it be?" He didn't hesitate. "Work on one thing at a time," he replied, "and get it right." Benjamin Franklin said much the same in 1771. In his *Autobiography*, he gives a masterly account of how to break a complex skill into its component behaviors and then how to work on improving it one behavior at a time. With authorities like Franklin and Landry to support me, I don't hesitate to put forward the first, and most important, principle for getting value from this book:

Start by picking *just one* behavior to practice. Don't move on to the next until you're confident you've got the first behavior right.

Rule 2: Try the New Behavior at Least Three Times

The first time you try anything new, it's bound to feel uncomfortable. It's not only new shoes that hurt at first.

Suppose, for example, you decide to practice Implication Questions. You're keeping Rule 1 in mind, so you're going to concentrate only on Implication Questions, not on the other behaviors we've covered. Off you go into a call. Do the new Implication Questions roll off your tongue in a smooth, convincing sequence? Not on your life! When you ask them you sound self-conscious, artificial, and awkward. And because of this, you don't make a particularly positive impression on the customer. After the call, if you're like most people we've trained, you're tempted to conclude that Implication Questions didn't help you sell—so you'd better drop them and try something different next call.

If you draw that conclusion, of course, you're making a big mistake. You have to try any new behavior several times before it becomes practiced enough to be both comfortable and effective. The new skill needs to be "broken in." It's not just in selling that this happens. Whenever you try to improve *any* skill, at first it feels awkward and it doesn't go right. I once asked a sample of 200 people, each of whom had taken golf lessons from a professional, whether their next round was better or worse. Out of the 200, 157 said that they scored *worse* after the lesson than before it.

What's the remedy? The principle which I use personally—and which Huthwaite recommends to those we train—is this:

Never judge whether a new behavior is effective until you've tried it *at least three times*.

Rule 3: Quantity Before Quality

Remember the old-fashioned way to learn a foreign language? You try to say a few words. "No," says your teacher, "that's the incorrect tense— you should be using a pluperfect." You try again. "Wrong," the teacher warns you, "you've got the tense right, but this is an irregular verb." With some nervousness you make a third attempt. "No," your teacher tells you, "this time the tense is right and the verb is right, but your pronunciation is terrible." Notice that every one of the teacher's comments is about the *quality* of your skill. Many of us struggled for years to learn a language this way. At the end of it we were able, hesitantly but correctly, to pronounce a few sentences with the right verbs, tenses, and word orders. Most of us never reached the point, despite several years of emphasis on quality, where we could speak the language confidently and comfortably.

In contrast, let's look at modern language training. Students are told, "Never mind about pronunciation, and don't worry about tenses. For now, word order doesn't matter and we don't care if you forget the differences between regular and irregular verbs. The only thing we want you to do is speak it, speak it, and speak it." The emphasis, in other words, is on quantity rather than quality—talking a *lot* is more important than talking *well*. Many convincing experiments have shown that this approach, which puts emphasis on the *quantity* of speech, can greatly speed the learning of language skills. At the end of a single year, students are talking the new language more confidently than those who have spent 5 times as long learning in the old quality-first manner. What's more surprising is that by talking the language a lot, the quality has improved too. In fact, the correctness of language, measured by pronunciation and grammar tests, is higher in those taught by the quantity approach than in those taught by the older quality methods. So in language training, at least, speaking it a lot wins hands down over speaking it well.

But does the same principle apply to a skill like selling? Yes—without question it does. Our studies have consistently shown that the fastest way to learn a new sales behavior is through using a quantity method. Let me give you an example of what I mean. There was a well-known multinational company whose name, for reasons of protecting the guilty, had better remain anonymous. This company liked the SPIN Model and wanted to produce a sales-training program based on it. The program's designers spent 9 months producing a $650,000 extravaganza that was meant to be the ultimate in sales training. *Quality* was their motto. So, for example, in their program you couldn't just ask Problem Questions. Oh no, that wouldn't do at all because you might not be asking the right *quality* of questions. Instead, they built a four-stage model of how to ask a Problem Question, with special attention to three ways in which Problem Questions could be smoothly linked to Situation Questions and with sundry other techniques to ensure that any Problem Question—when the poor student ultimately got round to asking it—would have the right quality. The result of their efforts was a 74-step sales model that was so demotivating and cumbersome that it didn't even get through its pilot without a walkout by confused and angry learners. Tracking students in the field afterward, we found that they were asking an average of 1.6 Problem Questions per call—no different from the pretraining level.

Huthwaite—maybe because we'd played no part in this monstrous design—was selected to be the bearer of ill tidings to corporate headquarters. I had to tell the decision maker that he'd just spent most of his training budget on a program which was so bad that it couldn't even stagger through its pilot test. When his initial rage had subsided to a gentle gibber, he was able to ask, "What shall I do?" We suggested that for considerably less than one-tenth of the cost, a program could be designed that would be much more effective. "Concentrate on *quantity*," we advised him, "and you'll get the results you're looking for." Sure enough, just 2 months later we had a program based on methods closely resembling effective language training. We didn't care whether questions were asked well or poorly, but we *did* care that people asked a lot of them. At the end of the training, in the final role plays, students were asking a dozen Problem Questions. Back out in the field, real-life responses from customers soon told them which of these questions worked best, and—as in language training—the quality improved dramatically. The $650,000 quality-based program was scrapped, and our cheap but effective quantity-based program was adopted in its place across the company's three largest divisions.

Exactly the same principle applies to your own selling when you're trying to learn a new behavior:

When you're practicing, concentrate on quantity: use a *lot* of the new behavior. Don't worry about quality issues, such as whether you're using it
smoothly or whether there might be a better way to phrase it. Those
things get in the way of effective skills learning. Use the new behavior
often enough and the quality will look after itself.

Rule 4: Practice in Safe Situations

I once ran a negotiating-skills program for company presidents. On the
last day, one of the participants asked me an innocent-sounding question. "Tomorrow," he explained, "I'll be going into the biggest negotiation of my career—I'm selling my company. What lessons from this
program should I concentrate on during the negotiation?" I think my
answer shocked him. "Forget every single thing you've heard on this
program," I advised him; "otherwise, you'll spend the rest of your life
regretting you came here."

Let me give you some similar advice. If you've just finished this book
and you're about to visit your most important account, then forget everything I've written. It's a strange quirk of human nature that we usually try to practice new skills in key situations, those important enough
to justify the effort of trying something new. This is a terrible mistake.
As we've seen, new skills are uncomfortable and awkward. They may
even have a negative effect on the customer. If you try them out in crucial situations, then you're likely to be unsuccessful. Suppose you've decided to ask more Need-payoff Questions. Don't practice on your biggest account. Instead, begin with small accounts, or with customers you
know well, or in areas where you've nothing to lose if you fail. In other
words:

**Always try out new behaviors in safe situations until they feel comfort-
able. Don't use important sales to practice new skills.**

These rules can be sequenced to provide a simple strategy for learning
or improving your skills (Figure 8.1). Although my purpose here is to
focus on improving selling skills, these four basic rules will help you improve *any* skills, from making love to flying airplanes.

A Summary of the Call Stages

Let's summarize the key points made in earlier chapters.

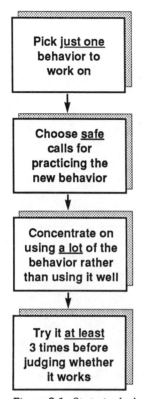

Figure 8.1. Strategies for learning a new skill.

Four Stages of a Sales Call
(Chapter 1)

Almost every sales call progresses through four distinct stages (Figure 8.2):

- *Preliminaries.* The warming-up events at the start of the call

- *Investigating.* Finding out facts, information, and needs

- *Demonstrating Capability.* Showing that you've got something worthwhile to offer

- *Obtaining Commitment.* Gaining an agreement to proceed to a further stage of the sale

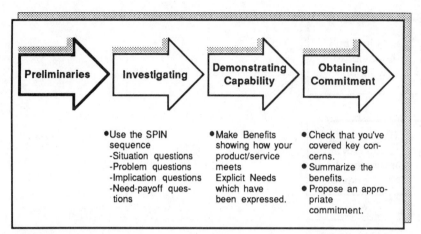

Figure 8.2. Call stages.

Preliminaries (Chapter 7)

We've suggested that there's no one best way to open a sales call. Successful people are flexible and rarely open two calls in the same way. The opening techniques recommended by traditional sales-training programs—(1) relating to the buyer's personal interests and (2) making an opening benefit statement—have unintended drawbacks and should be used with caution.

Investigating (Chapter 4)

Our research showed that the traditional distinction between open and closed questions doesn't predict success in larger sales. Instead, we discovered the SPIN sequence of questions that successful people use to uncover and develop customer needs in the larger sale:

- *Situation Questions.* About facts, background, and what the customer is doing now. Asking too many Situation Questions can bore or irritate the customer. Research shows that successful people ask them sparingly—so that each question has a purpose.
- *Problem Questions.* About the customer's problems, difficulties, or dissatisfactions. Problem Questions are strongly linked to success in smaller sales, but they are less powerful in major sales.
- *Implication Questions.* About the consequences or effects of a customer's problems. Successful calls usually contain a high level of Implication Questions. The ability to develop implications is a crucial

skill in the larger sale because it increases the customer's perception of *value* in the solution you offer.

- *Need-payoff Questions.* About the value, usefulness, or utility that the customer perceives in a solution. Like Implication Questions, Need-payoff Questions are strongly linked to success in the major sale.

The SPIN Model is often used sequentially, starting with Situation Questions to establish the background, then Problem Questions to uncover difficulties, then Implication Questions to develop the seriousness of a problem, and finally Need-payoff Questions to get the customer telling *you* the benefits of your solution. However, the SPIN sequence isn't a rigid formula. To be effective, it must be used flexibly.

Demonstrating Capability (Chapter 5)

The traditional definition of a Benefit—a statement that shows how your product can be used or can help the customer—works in small sales but fails as the sale grows larger. In major sales, the most effective type of Benefit shows how your product or service meets an Explicit Need expressed by the customer.

Obtaining Commitment (Chapter 2)

Closing techniques are effective in smaller sales, but they don't work in larger ones. Our studies showed that the simplest way to obtain commitment is also the most effective:

- *Check* that you've covered the buyer's key concerns.
- *Summarize* the Benefits.
- *Propose* an appropriate level of commitment.

A Strategy for Learning the SPIN Behaviors

My colleagues at Huthwaite have worked with many thousands of salespeople, helping them use the methods I've described in this book. We've experimented with dozens of different training approaches. In large corporations we've generally adopted designs that make very sophisticated use of advanced learning techniques. At the other extreme, we've also tried to develop some very simple ways to help individual salespeople improve their skills. Alas, there's no free lunch in the training business. It's an unfortunate truth that our more elaborate and sophisticated training designs have generally brought much better productivity gains than the simpler ones, and this has made us a little self-conscious about recommending simple steps for improving your skills.

Even so, there *are* some fairly easy, common-sense ways to take the research findings in this book and turn them into useful practice. We've found that people invariably find the following four pieces of implementation advice very helpful.

Focus on the Investigating Stage

Many people, when they plan calls, think about what they will *tell* the customer, not about what they will ask. They concentrate, in other words, on the Demonstrating Capability stage of the call. That's a mistake. However well you demonstrate capability, you'll have little impact unless you have first developed needs—so that the customer *wants* the capability you're offering. The same is true of the Obtaining Commitment stage; unless the customer wants what you have to offer, you're going to find it difficult to get a commitment. Focus your efforts on the Investigating stage. Practice your questioning skills, and the other stages of the call will generally look after themselves. If you know how to develop needs—to get your customers to *want* the capabilities you offer—then you'll have no problem showing Benefits or Obtaining Commitment. The key selling skill is in the Investigating stage, using the SPIN questions to get your customers to feel a genuine need for your product.

Develop Questions in the SPIN Sequence

Don't rush in to practice the high-powered Implication and Need-payoff Questions until you feel you have a solid and comfortable grasp of the simpler Situation and Problem Questions.

1. First decide whether you're asking enough questions of *any* type. If you've built up selling patterns that involve telling—in other words if you're giving a lot of Features and Advantages—then start by just asking more questions. Most of the questions you ask will be Situation Questions, but this is fine. Just keep asking questions for a few weeks until asking feels as comfortable as telling.

2. Next plan and ask Problem Questions. Aim, in the average call, to

ask a customer about problems, difficulties, and dissatisfactions at least half a dozen times. Concentrate on building up the *quantity* of your Problem Questions; don't worry about whether or not each question is a "good" one.

3. If you feel you're doing an effective job of uncovering customer problems, it's time to move on to Implication Questions. These are more difficult to ask, and you may need a couple of months' practice before you become entirely comfortable with Implication Questions. Plan them carefully.

A good starting point would be to reread the example transcript in the "Implication Questions" section of Chapter 4. Then, in place of the problem in the transcript, put in a problem of your own that one of your products could solve for your customer. Using the questions in the transcript as a model, try to write some examples of Implication Questions you could ask that would make your customer feel the problem is serious enough to justify action.. When I'm planning Implication Questions, I find it's useful to imagine a customer who's saying "So what? Yes, I've got that problem—but I don't think it's serious." I list the arguments I'd use to convince the customer that the problem really *is* serious—it's causing a loss of efficiency, it's increasing her costs, and it's demotivating her better people. Then I turn each of my arguments into a question—"What effect is the problem having on your efficiency?" and "How much is it increasing your costs?" and "What impact does it have on the motivation of your better people?"

4. Finally, when you're comfortable with Situation, Problem, and Implication Questions, turn your attention to Need-payoff Questions. Instead of giving Benefits to the customer, concentrate on asking questions that get the customer to tell *you* the Benefits. Ask questions like these:

How would that help you?

What do *you* see as the pluses of this approach?

Is there any other way our product could be useful?

Again, don't worry about whether you're asking Need-payoff Questions *well*. Concentrate on quantity—on asking *lots* of them.

Analyze Your Product in Problem-Solving Terms

Stop thinking about your products in terms of their Features and Advantages. Instead, think of each product in terms of its problem-solving capabilities. Analyze products by listing the problems they are designed to solve. Then use your list to plan questions you can use in calls. By thinking of your products this way, you'll find it easier to adopt a SPIN questioning style.

Plan, Do, and *Review*

The majority of salespeople acknowledge the importance of call planning even if, in reality, their planning is no more than a few moments of anxiety before the call. However, only limited learning comes from planning the call, or from making it. The most important lessons come from the way you *review* the calls you make. After each call, ask yourself such questions as these:

- Did I achieve my objectives?
- If I were making the call again, what would I do differently?
- What have I learned that will influence future calls on this account?
- What have I learned that I can use elsewhere?

Unfortunately, few of us take enough time to ask ourselves questions like these systematically. Over the years I've had the opportunity to travel with dozens of the world's top salespeople—and as a researcher, I've looked for any differences that distinguish them from those who haven't made it to the top. Two differences stand out. The first is that the top people I've traveled with put great emphasis on reviewing each call—dissecting what they've learned and thinking about possible improvement.

The second difference is that most of the really successful salespeople I've studied recognize that their success depends on getting *details* right. They may have excellent skills in terms of broad, large-scale strategic account planning, but this is not what distinguishes them. Many of the less successful people I've studied can give an impeccable account of themselves in terms of overall strategy. The difference that's so evident in top people is that they can translate strategy into effective sales behavior—they know what to *do* in the call. They understand details, which may be why they put such emphasis on planning and reviewing each call.

It's worth asking yourself whether you are giving enough time to reviewing the details of what happened in the call. Never be content with global conclusions like "it went quite well." Ask yourself about the *details*. Did some parts of the call go better than others? Why? Which *spe-*

cific questions you asked had the most influence on the customer? Which needs did the customer feel strongly? Which needs changed during the discussion? Why? Which of the behaviors you used had the most impact? Unless you analyze your selling on this level of detail, you'll miss important opportunities for learning and improving your selling skills.

A Final Word

Perhaps the most significant conclusion I've come to from Huthwaite's research studies of selling is about the importance of details. Many years ago, at the start of our research, I would have told you that sales success lay in the broader areas. I would have chosen global factors like personality, attitudes, interpersonal chemistry, or overall account strategy to explain why one person sold better than another. I don't believe this anymore. Increasingly our research has shown that success is constructed from those important little building blocks called behaviors. More than anything else, it's the hundreds of minute behavioral details in a call that will decide whether it succeeds.

I'm not the first to come to the conclusion that success rests on understanding the minute details. In 1801 William Blake wrote:

> He who would do good to another must do it in Minute Particulars.
> General Good is the plea of the scoundrel, hypocrite, and flatterer;
> For Art and Science cannot exist but in minutely organized particulars.

So, as a parting word, let me urge you to concentrate on those minute particulars. Give real attention to the basic building-block behaviors you use when you sell. We've put thousands of sales calls under the microscope to isolate some of the detailed behavioral elements that bring success in the major sale. Use the results of our research to examine, develop, and improve the minute particulars of your selling skills.

Appendix A

Evaluating the SPIN Model

More than a century ago Lord Kelvin wrote, "If you cannot measure it—if you cannot express it in quantitative terms—then your knowledge is of a meagre and insignificant kind." How right he was! But alas, today we live in an age that has lost the exuberance of the great nineteenth-century scientific investigators. Measurement, proof, and careful testing don't generate the same excitement that they did in the golden age of science. As a result, our work on testing the validity of the SPIN Model gets relegated to an appendix like this instead of being bang in the middle of the book where Lord Kelvin would have put it.

If you're the one person in a hundred who bothers to read the appendix in a book like this, then you deserve my admiration and gratitude. Personally, I find the material here to be the most exciting part of our work. I hope you'll find it rewarding too.

My topic is an intriguing one—proof. How do we know that the methods I've described in this book really contribute to sales success? This has been the most difficult challenge in our research—collecting solid evidence that the ideas we've developed really bring a measurable improvement in bottom-line sales results. As far as I can tell, we're the first research team to bring rigorous scientific methods to establishing whether particular selling skills result in measurable productivity improvement.

Many people, of course, have made *claims* that their models and methods bring dramatic improvements in sales results. As I look through my junk mail today, there are several enticing promises of success. "Double your sales," claims a 1-day program. "At last," says another, "a proven method that will increase your sales by up to 300 percent." A third offering tells me, "After this program, the sales of our

161

Branch went through the roof. Yours will too!" Yes, there's no shortage of *claims* made by training programs that their methods bring measurable improvement. But how many of these dramatic cases stand up to close scrutiny? None that I've looked at. Unfortunately, when you examine them closely, most of the heavily advertised "miracle cures" in sales training look remarkably similar to the claims made for snake oil a couple of hundred years ago.

I'm not being unduly malicious when I draw parallels between sales training and snake oil. Many of the purveyors of snake oil, miracle mixtures, and wonder medicines sincerely believed that they had found a great cure. Their sincerity was based on a simple misperception. Put yourself in the shoes of an eighteenth-century country doctor. You're treating a very ill patient. You've tried everything, yet nothing seems to work. So, in desperation, you put together a mixture of herbs and potions. Your patient takes the mixture and recovers. Eureka! Your medicine works; you've found a miracle cure. What you don't see, in your enthusiasm, is that the patient was getting better anyway. For the rest of your life you honestly believe it was your mixture that caused the recovery.

That's exactly what happens with most sales training. The designer puts together a mixture of concepts and models—and administers it in the form of a training program. Afterward there's an increase in sales. So, in all sincerity, the training designer concludes that the training has *caused* the increase. I spent 3 years doing postgraduate research into training evaluation. Over and over again I'd come across this miracle-cure phenomenon. I recall, for example, a trainer from a large chemical company telling me that he had a program that doubled sales. Sure enough, he had figures to prove his point—the sales of his division had risen by 118 percent since the training. On looking closely at the curriculum, however, I found it was little different from the training that his division had been running for years. I couldn't find anything to justify a sudden 118 percent increase in sales. But looking at the *market* told a different story. A large competitor had gone out of business because of industrial disputes, new products had been introduced, and prices had changed. On top of that, there were several significant changes in sales-force management and policy—not to mention a major advertising campaign. It's reasonable to suppose that each of these factors had a much larger impact on sales than a conventional sales-training program did. In my judgment, the patient would have recovered without the miracle cure—the training was snake oil.

During my evaluation research I investigated many claims for sales increases resulting from training. More than 90 percent of them could be accounted for more easily by other management or market factors.

There are so many variables that affect sales performance—and training is just one factor. In almost every case we studied, there was a more plausible reason for the increase. I'm not doubting the sincerity of those who tell you how their wonderful sales method has doubled results. But as with any miracle cure, you've got to ask whether the patient would have done equally well without the medicine.

Correlations and Causes

Whether we're talking about medicine or training, it's extremely difficult to prove that one's "cure" is effective. Yet that's a difficulty I now face in this chapter, because the question I want to answer for you is "Does this stuff work?" What's the evidence that the ideas we've put forward here will make a worthwhile contribution to your sales results? If you're going to invest time and effort in practicing the sales skills I've described, you'll need to know that I'm offering you more than snake oil. But how can I *prove* to you that the SPIN process increases sales?

Let me start with how *not* to do it (Figure A.1). In the early days of the SPIN Model we were working with a capital goods company based just outside New York. The training staff were anxious to test whether the model brought improved sales results. They measured the average monthly sales for the 28 people they trained. For the 6 months before training, the average sales were 3.1 orders per month. But in the 6 months after the training, the average sales rose to 4.9 orders per month—an increase of 58 percent.

Can we conclude that the SPIN Model increases orders by 58 percent? This would be a very unwise conclusion. Let's look more closely at the result. In the 6 months following the program, two important new products were introduced. Sales territories were redrawn, and 23 of the 28 trained people were given larger territories with greater sales potential. Company sales increased during this time by approximately 35 percent—and most of this increase came from *untrained* people. As we looked more closely, it became clear that we were in danger of kidding ourselves that SPIN was a miracle cure when, in reality, we had no way to tell what part of the increase was due to SPIN and what part resulted from other factors.

In the same vein, I have to advise you not to be taken in by this glowing little report of another SPIN evaluation. This one is from Honeywell's *Management Magazine:*

> Our European sales force was oriented primarily to product and short-cycle selling. We needed a truly effective program...that could be applied

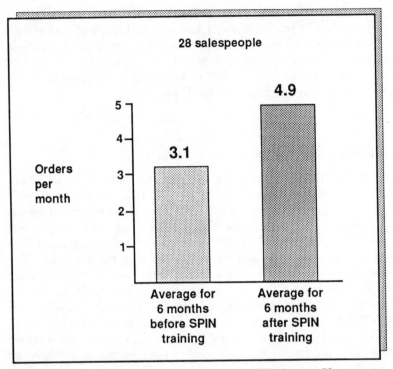

Figure A.1. A misleading example of improvement: SPIN brings a 58 percent increase in orders ... or does it?

universally to our varied European markets. Late in 1978 the SPIN program was adapted into all European languages. There was a 20% increase in sales success...which may rise higher as the salesmen sharpen their SPIN techniques.

Yes, following the implementation of the SPIN approach there was a 20 percent increase in sales. But what this report *doesn't* tell you is that Honeywell introduced a number of important new products to Europe that year, including the revolutionary TDC 2000 process control system. It's quite possible that the products created the whole increase. In Honeywell's case there's no way we can tell whether the SPIN approach is any improvement on snake oil.

Control Groups

The most serious weakness of results like these is that the trainers didn't set up a control group—a matched group of *untrained* people who could provide a baseline against which changes in the performance of the trained group could be judged. I imagine that the majority of readers will know about control groups and how important they are for any experimental work. But you may not know that much of the early use of control groups was in medicine, where they were used in an attempt to sort out whether a cure was genuine or just snake oil. If the trainers had set up a control group of 28 matched, untrained salespeople, we could have compared the performance of the two groups to obtain a truer picture.

But even with a control group, results can be misleading. Here's a study that seems, on the surface, a very convincing test of whether the SPIN Model brings improved performance in major sales.

The Case of the Plausible Explanation. A large multinational company decided to test the SPIN Model by training a whole major-account branch of 31 salespeople. As a control, it chose other branches that were not given the training. If the trained branch improved more than the others, then this wouldn't be due to the market or the products because these factors applied equally to both the control and the experimental branches. Even more important, there were no significant changes in people—the branch had unusually low turnover at the sales and management levels. Perhaps, this time, we had a valid test of whether the SPIN approach brings productivity.

The results, a 57 percent gain compared with the control group, certainly look convincing (Figure A.2). But we have to ask the standard evaluator's question: "Is there any other equally plausible way to explain this increase?" Unfortunately for us, there is. The branch had been created very recently—just 4 months before the SPIN training. The average selling cycle for the product range was 3 months. So the productivity improvement could well have been caused by the time required for a new branch to get up to speed, coupled with the delayed effects of a 3-month sales cycle. Once again, our "proof" can be explained away.

In our research files, we've many similar examples of evaluation studies that look plausible at a first glance but don't stand up to close scrutiny. Here's one more case to make the point.

Foiled Again. A large business-machines company decided to evaluate the SPIN methods in a seasonal market where February was a peak month. In order to compensate for seasonal and market effects, it used as control groups every other branch that operated in the same market. The company tracked the order record of each branch before and after the experimental branch was trained in early January. As can be seen in Figure A.3, the SPIN-trained branch showed an impressive productiv-

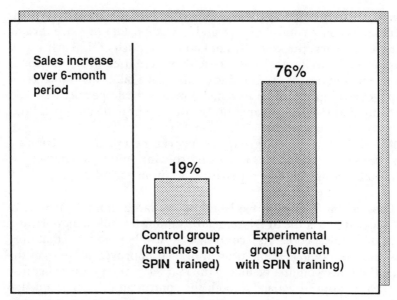

Figure A.2. A misleading control-group study.

ity gain compared with the others. This time, unlike our earlier studies, all five branches were well established—so there wasn't a problem about the selling cycle or the learning curve. Could this be the proof we'd been looking for? Unfortunately, it wasn't.

In November the branch manager had changed. How do we know whether the dramatic improvement in productivity was caused by the SPIN Model or by the new sales-activity management system introduced in December? The question is unanswerable. Nevertheless, the company attempted an answer of sorts by interviewing all participating salespeople. They asked each person to estimate how much of the change was due to the SPIN training and how much to other causes. Although everybody obligingly gave an estimate, the fact that their most common response was that 50 percent was due to SPIN makes me suspicious. Whenever people reply, "50 percent," to any question about causes, I interpret this as meaning that they haven't a clue.

Failure after Failure

You can never entirely eliminate the effects of other organizational and market factors—which means that it's extremely difficult to obtain convincing proof of any selling model. Heaven knows, we've tried. We got

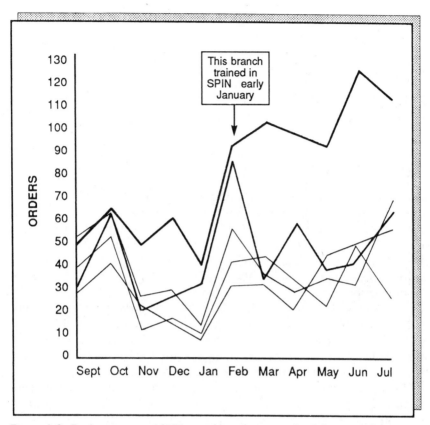

Figure A.3. Productivity gain of SPIN-trained branch compared with four control groups.

one organization to agree not to change products, management, or salespeople for the whole of a 6-month test period. For a while we were convinced that we had an evaluation study that would stand up to the toughest scrutiny. Then, just as we were moving smoothly into the third month of the test, the wretched competition cut its prices by 15 percent. Our client, forced to respond quickly, changed prices, people, and product introductions. Another test ruined!

We *thought* we finally had all the important factors under control in a high-tech company. The test branch was doing well—73 percent ahead of the control branches—and this time we were convinced we had a winner. Halfway through the test, however, we fell victim to one of the branch managers from the control group. Before the test, he'd been top branch and proud of it. But now, seeing that the test-branch figures were looking much better than his own, he decided to take action. In the dead of night he raided the training department's files and made a copy of all the program materials we'd used with the test branch. Returning home with his loot, he swore all his salespeople to secrecy and ran his own training classes using the stolen material.

It ruined our test. Although I was furious at the time, looking back I can't help thinking it's the most convincing evaluation study of all when your methods are good enough for a sales manager to drive 600 miles in the middle of the night to steal them.

Is Proof Possible?

In 1970 I wrote a book on training evaluation with Peter Warr and Mike Bird. One of our conclusions was that the difficulties involved in controlling real-life variables made it almost impossible to prove that training increased productivity. While we were writing the book, we discussed an "ideal" evaluation study. Mike Bird and I shared an office and we spent hours thinking about how we would set about designing the perfect piece of evaluation.

"If you look at it simply," Mike said, "the way most people set about evaluation is like this." He drew a picture on the blackboard (Figure A.4). "But," he added, "look at all the complicating variables. How can you possibly prove whether any change is due to training?" He quickly sketched in some of the other factors (Figure A.5).

This was turning into a depressing conversation, because I'd just been reading Karl Popper, the philosopher who's best known for suggesting that you can't prove *anything*. What Popper had suggested is that the only way science can "prove" something is by continually trying to *disprove* it and failing. "Could we adopt that kind of approach?" I asked. "Just suppose that instead of trying to prove that training brings productivity, we attacked the problem from the other end and tried to *disprove* any productivity effect. Would that be better?"

We didn't take the conversation further—but years later, as I wrestled with the problems of testing whether our SPIN approach worked, I remembered that discussion with Mike. Should we forget about proof

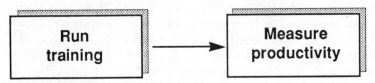

Figure A.4. The usual way of evaluating sales training.

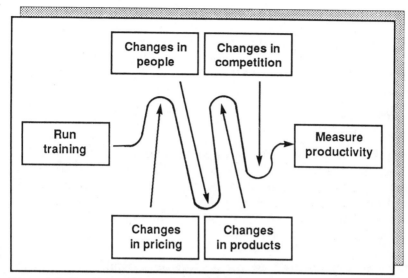

Figure A.5. Variables complicating accurate measurement.

and instead set about *disproving* the idea that the skills described in this book cause more sales?

Proof or Disproof—Does It Matter?

As a practical person, you may find my researcher's obsession with proof or disproof to be an academic form of overkill. In my defense I'd say that many billions of dollars are being wasted each year, teaching selling methods without one scrap of proof to show whether or not they work. No other area of business is so casual about testing its products or methods. Civilized society would collapse if manufacturing design showed the same lack of concern with product effectiveness that I see in most training-design organizations. Just because it's difficult to measure the effectiveness of a sales approach doesn't mean we shouldn't try. On the contrary, the difficulties make it all the more important. Without honest attempts at better measurement of sales-training effectiveness, we'll continue to waste billions of dollars that could be spent more productively elsewhere. I don't really care whether the emphasis is on proof or disproof. But I *do* passionately support anything that will give better measurement and testing, because without these tests, my profession is in the snake-oil business.

If you'll forgive me a moment of preaching, I hope you'll see this concern with thorough evaluation as being in *your* interest. Our reason for all these measurements and tests is that we're trying to make sure that what we give you will work. There used to be an old army saying: "If it moves, shoot it, and if it doesn't move, paint it." Huthwaite's equivalent is: "If it moves, measure it, and if you can't measure it, shoot it." Measurement and testing is almost an obsession with us.

Stages of Disproof

In pursuit of our enthusiasm for a rigorous measurement of the SPIN approach, my Huthwaite colleagues and I spent unreasonable amounts of time struggling with the problems of proof and disproof (Figure A.6). We decided that before we looked at productivity gains (Test 3), we first needed to pass two other tests—or opportunities for disproof, as Popper would have called them.

Test 1: Do These Skills Make Calls More Successful?   How did we know we were teaching the right things? Before we could begin to answer elaborate questions about productivity change, we needed first to test whether the models worked. For example, suppose we were teaching a major-account team a traditional low-value sales model that involved asking open and closed questions, giving Advantages, and then using closing techniques to gain commitment. From the evidence we've presented so far, it's not likely that adopting this model would make major-account sales calls more successful. Even if there were substantial productivity gains after the training, they would probably have been caused by other factors. So before we started to measure productivity gains, our first test had to establish whether we were teaching the right things.

Generically, we knew that the SPIN Model passed this test because it was derived from studies of successful calls. So there was a high probability that if we taught the SPIN skills, we would be teaching something that would make calls more successful. But if we wanted to design the ultimate evaluation study, we'd have to go beyond this. We'd have to answer a very *specific* question about the individual salespeople whose productivity we intended to measure. We couldn't rely on studies we'd done in other companies, in other markets, or with other groups. What if this group was different? How did we know that just because SPIN worked somewhere else, it would work here? In the ultimate evaluation test we would start by doing some research to establish what a successful call looks like *for the group of people we're going to train*. We wouldn't take the chance that unique factors in terms of their geography, market, products, or sales organization might invalidate our results. If, from this

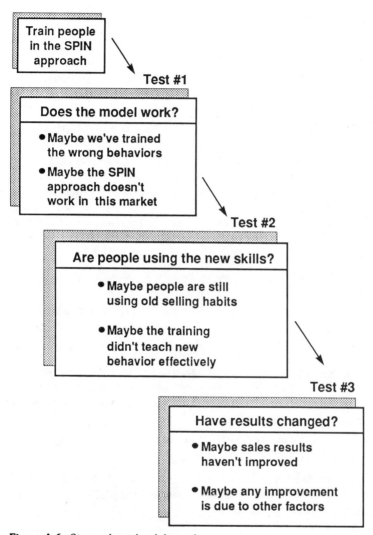

Figure A.6. Stages of proof and disproof.

first test, we could collect solid evidence that the things we were teaching worked for this set of individuals, then we would have eliminated one more source of disproof.

Test 2: How Do We Know That People Are Using the New Skills? The next test in our quest for disproof would be to discover whether people were actually using the new skills in real calls after the training. I was once caught out on this test. We were measuring productivity improvement in a group of salespeople from a division of General Electric. In the 6 months after the SPIN-based training, sales had risen by an average of 18 percent. Could we claim the credit? Alas, no. By watching these people sell before and after the training, we established that they weren't using significantly more of the SPIN behaviors afterward than they were before we trained them. Once again we had disproved that the productivity gain should be credited to us.

This test, which measures whether the training has made people behave any differently in their calls, is rarely if ever carried out by training designers. It's a pity. We've learned a lot about effective training design by analyzing the amount of behavior change our programs have caused. I'm sure that other designers would also find this kind of measurement more useful than the usual smiles test—"the training must be good because people say they liked it"—which is the normal extent of training evaluation.

An Evaluation Plan

Bit by bit we were developing a specification for a very sophisticated and thorough method that we could use to evaluate the effectiveness of our SPIN Model. The evaluation steps would be:

1. Watch a group of major-account salespeople in action to find out whether there are more SPIN behaviors used in their successful calls than in the calls that fail. If so, we've passed Test 1; we now know that the model works for this group of people.

2. Train the group to use the SPIN methods that we're trying to evaluate.

3. Go out with each person in the group after the training to discover whether they're now using more of the trained behaviors during their calls. If so, we've passed Test 2; we know that people are actually using the new skills.

4. Assuming that we pass on Test 1 and Test 2, measure the productivity gain compared with control groups as Test 3.

It seems an elaborate method, but we didn't see any alternative. We searched for a simpler answer, but none of the usual superficial evaluation tests stood up to close examination. The author and corporate planning expert Michael Kami once told me, "For every complex question, there is a simple answer—and it is wrong." We were forced to agree with him. If we wanted a solid evaluation of a complex problem, we'd have to accept a difficult method for getting there.

A Test with Kodak—Almost

We took our evaluation plan to a number of clients and tried to interest them in it. This is a polite way of saying that we tried to get them to pay for a very expensive test. Most of them, realizing how costly the test would be, encouraged us to take our evaluation elsewhere. For a time we had high hopes of a full test with Kodak—an organization with a long tradition of careful testing of new methods. Kodak was considering using SPIN-based training worldwide across all its divisions involved in major sales. An evaluation test seemed a sensible first step. We agreed to test the model by observing a group of salespeople from Kodak's Health Sciences Division. Sure enough, the SPIN Model worked exactly as our research had predicted. Implication and Need-payoff Questions were more than twice as frequent in successful calls as in the ones that failed.

Next we trained the pilot group and, after the training, went out to observe whether its people were using the new skills. Once again, things looked good. Benefits had trebled, Implication Questions had trebled, and Need-payoff Questions had doubled. The people were now using more of the successful behaviors than they were before the training.

We were delighted. For the first time we were about to begin a productivity test where we could say, "We *know* the model works and we *know* these people are using it in their calls." Then came one of those good news, bad news bombshells. The good news was that Kodak was so happy with the pilot test that it had decided to adopt the SPIN methods worldwide. The bad news was that Kodak was so convinced by its people's reactions to the pilot that it saw no point in elaborate and costly productivity tests. The "smiles test" had stabbed us in the back!

Enter Motorola Canada

We were just remarking to ourselves that the evaluator's lot was one of unrelieved woe when we had an offer we couldn't refuse from Motorola. Like Kodak, Motorola wanted to test the SPIN Model with the intention, if it worked, of adopting it worldwide. Its chosen test group was the Communications Division of Motorola Canada. This time we were careful to set the evaluation study in concrete well before the project, so that none of our tests would escape. As an added bonus, Motorola hired an independent evaluator, Marti Bishop, who had worked with our models and methods in her previous job as Evaluation Manager in the Xerox Corporation. Her function was to test the effectiveness of the SPIN program rigorously, going through the full steps we had outlined for the ideal productivity evaluation.

I now quote from a condensed version of her report:

Motorola Canada Productivity Study

This report is a productivity analysis of the SPIN program that was conducted during the third quarter of 1981.
    It sets out to answer these questions:

q Does the SPIN Model work in Motorola Canada?

q Are people using the model after the training?

q Has this led to measurable improvement in their productivity?

Does the Model Work?

Motorola's first concern is to test whether the SPIN behaviors predict success in Motorola's sales calls in the way that they have proved successful in other companies.
    To test this, we traveled with each of the 42 sales reps who were to be trained and analyzed the frequency of the SPIN behaviors in their successful and unsuccessful calls. We found that all SPIN behaviors were at a higher frequency in the successful calls:

	Successful calls
Situation Questions	1% more
Problem Questions	17% more*
Implication Questions	53% more*
Need-payoff Questions	60% more*
Benefits	64% more*
Features	5% more

*indicates item is statistically significant

The SPIN training concentrated on developing an increased number of Problem Questions, Implication Questions, Need-payoff Questions, and Benefits. As each of these behaviors is at a significantly higher frequency in Motorola Canada's successful calls, we can conclude that the training is teaching people behaviors that should help them sell more effectively.

Have People Changed?

There's evidence that the model works in Motorola. The next step must be to show that the 42 people who were trained are actually using the new behaviors in their calls. To test this, we observed people selling before the training period, during the training period, and after it in order to determine whether they are now behaving differently with their customers.
    We sampled each of the 42 people at five points (Figure A.7). The first time we went out with them was immediately before the training. The other four times were at intervals of approximately 3 weeks during the training period itself. At the start of the training, people were asking more Situation Questions (average 8.6 per call) than the combined total of Problem *plus*

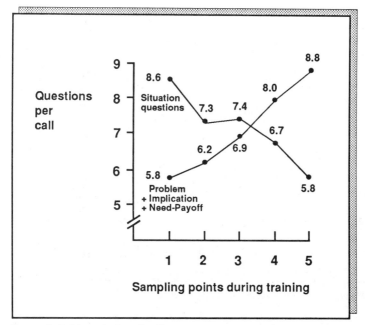

Figure A.7. Motorola Canada: Changes in questioning behavior.

Implication *plus* Need-payoff Questions (average 5.8 per call). So the three questioning behaviors statistically associated with success were being used less than Situation Questions—the one questioning behavior *not* significantly associated with success.

By the end of the training period, however, this had been reversed. The frequency of the successful questions had risen to 8.8 in the average call, while the level of Situation Questions had fallen. In terms of questioning behavior, we can safely conclude that the 42 salespeople are now behaving in a more successful way than before.

At the start of the training, the Benefits were at an average level of 1.2 per call (Figure A.8). By the end of the training, Benefits rose to 2.2 per call. Remember that Benefits, of all the behaviors, are the ones most predictive of success in Motorola Canada calls. Your salespeople are now giving customers almost twice as many Benefits per call as they were before the training. In view of this, it would not be surprising if this pilot results in measurable sales increases.

Has Productivity Changed?

To measure productivity change, I have:

■ Examined the sales results for the 42 people in the pilot and compared them with a control group of 42 untrained salespeople from Motorola Canada.

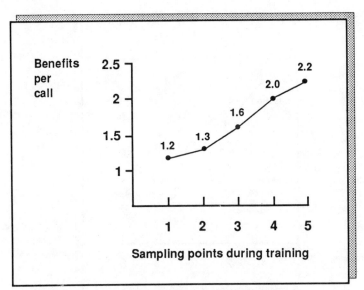

Figure A.8. Motorola Canada: Changes in Benefits per call.

- Compared the results for three time periods:
  - Three months *before* the SPIN training
  - Three months *during* the SPIN implementation period
  - Three months *after* the implementation
- The results therefore span a 9-month period.
- Measured sales in terms of:
  - Total orders
  - Orders from new accounts
  - Orders from existing accounts
  - Dollar value of sales

In terms of total orders (Figure A.9), the 42 people in the control group have shown a 13 percent fall from their original pretraining level. This is due to the competitiveness of the communications marketplace, coupled with the extremely difficult Canadian economy. In contrast, the SPIN-trained group has shown a 17 percent gain, reversing the trends of a difficult market. This gross difference of 30 percent in order rate between the control and experimental groups is statistically significant.

The management of Motorola Canada is focusing its effort on increasing new business and wants to know whether the SPIN training made a significant contribution to new-business sales. As Figure A.10 shows,

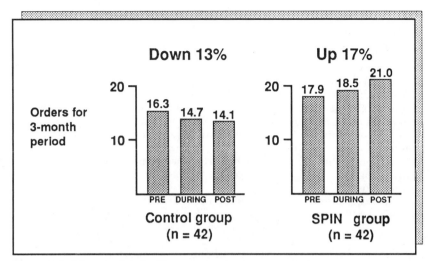

Figure A.9. Motorola Canada: Changes in total order levels.

new-business sales from the control group increased only during the training period, when the sales organization was putting great effort into new-business sales; in the period after the training, sales fell back to below their original level, reflecting the difficulties in the market. In contrast, the SPIN-trained group showed an order gain of 63 percent, reversing the generally poor market performance. It's particularly interesting to note the increase in the SPIN-trained group's orders in the period *after* the training

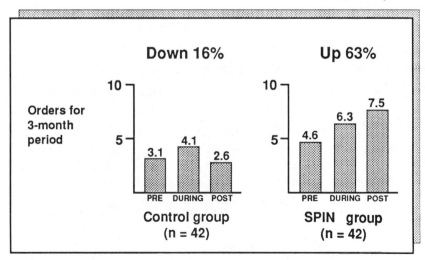

Figure A.10. Motorola Canada: Changes in new-business orders.

had ended; this suggests that the new skills are now self-maintaining and can be expected to make a continued impact on sales productivity. Before the study, some of your sales managers had expressed reservations about the "soft" nature of the SPIN Model, with its emphasis on probing and not on the "hard" closing techniques that some managers felt to be essential to the new business sale in a very difficult and competitive market, but the results indicate that they have no reason to be worried. The SPIN training has succeeded in generating significant business against hard-sell competition.

In terms of business generated from existing accounts (Figure A.11), the record of the control group is better. Both groups show a fall in business from existing accounts during the training. This is due to the sales organization's focus on new business during that period. However, while the control group shows a 13 percent overall decline, the SPIN-trained group shows a 1 percent increase.

An increase in orders can be misleading. It's possible that the productivity gain of the SPIN group was because it took more small orders, while the control group took fewer orders but each one had a greater dollar value. Because of this possibility, we needed to take a direct measurement of the dollar value of sales. Since dollar sales figures are confidential and this is a report for general release, we have therefore displayed the change in dollar value for the two groups in percentage terms to preserve confidentiality (Figure A.12). The control group showed a decline of 22.1 percent in terms of dollars sold; again, this reflects the extraordinarily difficult market conditions. The SPIN-trained group reversed this trend, showing an overall gain of 5.3 percent in dollar value. Note that these results suggest that some of the dramatic 63 percent order increase made by the SPIN group in the new-business area does come from a larger number of smaller orders.

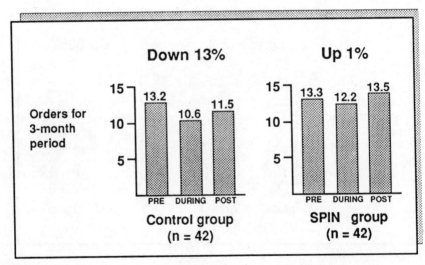

Figure A.11. Motorola Canada: Changes in orders from existing customers.

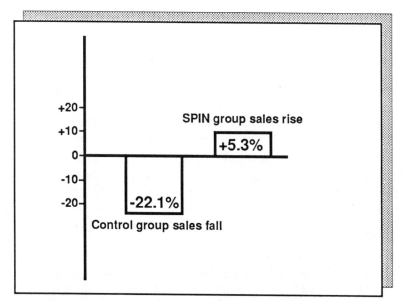

Figure A.12. Motorola Canada: Pre/post change in dollar value of sales.

In terms of dollar sales, the SPIN group is running at 27.4 percent above the control group. This difference is substantial and statistically significant. It would seem that the cost and effort of implementing the SPIN approach has been repaid many times over in terms of sales results.

Conclusions

These results suggest that the SPIN approach has succeeded in:

- Changing the skill levels of the people trained
- Increasing order levels, particularly in the new-business area
- Increasing the dollar volume of sales by an average of 27 percent above the control group

Two Serious Flaws

Marti Bishop's evaluation study represented the most detailed, rigorous, and comprehensive examination of a sales-training program ever carried out. I've quoted here from the summary version, but it's just the tip of the iceberg. She used additional control groups, used methodologies involving sales managers in the data collection process, and used some sophisticated computer techniques to build success models and analyze results. But as powerful as this study is, it still doesn't contain that elusive "proof" we were looking for.

If I wanted to discredit the Motorola study, I'd point out two flaws, each of which could be potentially serious enough to give a strict methodologist palpitations:

1. The control group starts from a lower point than the SPIN group. If you look at order levels before training (Figure A.9), the control group averaged 16.3 orders and the SPIN group 17.9. Now this difference isn't statistically significant, so perhaps it's nothing to worry about. Nevertheless, a cynic might argue that the SPIN group did better in a difficult economy because it was a little better to begin with.

2. There might be a *Hawthorne effect*. This is a technical term for the artificial increase in results that you get when you pay attention to people. The name comes from the Hawthorne plant of Western Electric, where some of the early productivity studies were carried out in the late 1920s. In one of the Hawthorne experiments, researchers found that when they increased the intensity of the plant's lighting, productivity rose. But to their astonishment, productivity also rose when they *decreased* the lighting levels. Their conclusion was that you can get a short-term increase in productivity just by giving people attention. In the Motorola study, you could argue, the productivity increase came from all the training attention that the SPIN group was receiving. It wouldn't matter whether we trained the group in the SPIN methods or in aerobic dancing. Productivity would have risen anyway because of the Hawthorne effect.

I had a couple of standard answers prepared to counter any suggestion that the change was due to a Hawthorne effect. My first defense was that Hawthorne effects are much less common than most people suppose and that when they do occur, they are short-term, usually lasting for a matter of days at the most. The Motorola study, which spanned a 9-month evaluation period, would almost certainly be free of any serious Hawthorne effect. My second defense was: "Who cares? The fact is that we've increased productivity. If it's a Hawthorne effect, then let's Hawthorne the whole sales force and get a 30 percent increase in sales from everybody." But my heart wasn't in either of these answers. The researcher in me badly wanted to know whether a Hawthorne effect existed and, if so, how much it had contributed to the productivity gain.

A New Evaluation Test

Motorola was convinced enough by the study to adopt the SPIN methods worldwide. Being satisfied that the methods worked, it saw no value in further attempts to *disprove* the link between SPIN and productivity. In fact, Motorola dismissed my concern as an example of that rather quaint eccentricity which the English show in times of stress.

We needed a new client with enough doubt to justify another large-scale investigation. Salvation came in the form of a giant multinational business-machines company who, like Motorola, wished to test SPIN for worldwide application. With only moderate difficulty, I persuaded the company to let me carry out the remaining two tests that would plug the gaps in the Motorola study: (1) using a matched control group and (2) measuring the Hawthorne effect.

Before carrying out these tests, we went through the same methodology that we had used in Motorola. I'll spare you the detailed findings, which were very similar to those in Motorola except for these differences:

- Situation Questions were 4 percent *lower* in successful calls. This is in line with our main research findings, which show that Situation Questions have a slightly negative effect on customers.

- As in Motorola, the Problem, Implication, and Need-payoff Questions were all significantly higher in successful calls. So were the Benefits. (But unlike Motorola, where Need-payoff Questions were the ones most strongly associated with success, the most powerful behavior in this study turned out to be Implication Questions.)

The behavioral changes brought about by the training were greater in this implementation than in Motorola. As Figure A.13 shows, the Problem, Implication, and Need-payoff Questions almost doubled, while the level of Situation Questions remained fairly constant.

The Benefits showed a particularly pleasing rise—from 1.1 per call to 3.4 (Figure A.14). This may not sound like much, but here's how I looked at it. The 55 people trained in the study were making an average of 16 sales call per week, which means that in an average week before the SPIN training there were 968 Benefits offered to customers. At the end of the study, in an average week the same people were giving 2992 Benefits. It would be surprising *not* to get a significant increase in sales from these 2024 extra Benefits.

A Matched Control Group

Our opportunity in this study to match the control group with the experimental group so that both groups started with the same order level allowed us to test one possible weakness in our Motorola results—that the reason for the increase could be because the SPIN group started from a higher point. Again, as in Motorola, we compared the perfor-

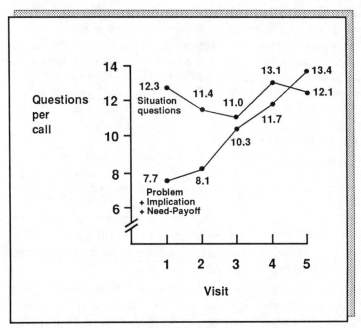

Figure A.13. Changes in questioning behavior.

mance of each group for a 3-month *pre* period and a 3-month *post* period. The control group showed a 21 percent fall in orders, while the SPIN group showed a 16 percent gain under the same, unfavorable economic and competitive conditions (Figure A.15). This study was also carried out under unfavorable economic and competitive conditions, which accounts for the fall in the control group's orders.

By having matched the initial order levels of the control and experimental groups, we could now confidently reject the idea that the reason for Motorola's 30 percent gain in orders was that the SPIN group had better salespeople to begin with. That explanation couldn't be true here, where the initial order levels of both groups were the same.

Measuring the Hawthorne Effect

The Hawthorne effect was harder to test. As far as we knew, nobody before us had ever tried to measure whether a Hawthorne element existed in sales training. As we thought about the problem, it became easy to see why we were the first. It's not hard to measure the impact of plant lighting on output, but how do you measure whether a sales productiv-

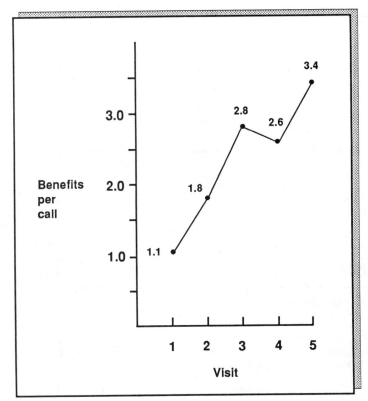

Figure A.14. Changes in benefits.

ity gain is due to the SPIN Model or due simply to the fact that you've given attention to people by offering them training?

The method we adopted was a little complex, but this was inevitable, given the difficulty of the issue we were trying to measure. Basically, the approach we used was this:

1. We reanalyzed the productivity results from our group of 55 people trained to use the SPIN approach. Each of these people had exactly the same number of hours of training, so all 55 had received a similar level of attention. All had, so to speak, an identical dose of the Hawthorne effect.

2. We divided our 55 people into two subgroups. In any group that's learning any skill—whether it's golf, a foreign language, or selling— some people naturally learn more than others. From having measured their behavior in calls, we identified the 27 people who were displaying the most use of the SPIN behaviors and put them in one

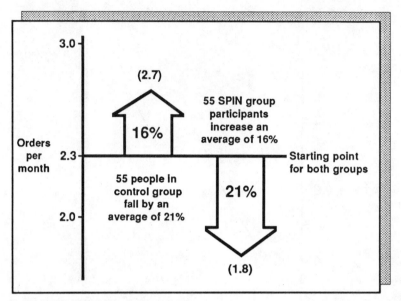

Figure A.15. Changes in productivity after training.

subgroup, and in the other subgroup we put the other 28, whose use of the SPIN behaviors was lower.

3. We compared the sales results of the two subgroups. If their productivity gains had been due entirely to a Hawthorne effect, then both subgroups should have shown identical gains, because both had received the same amount of training and management attention. But, if their productivity gains had resulted from using the SPIN Model, then the subgroup showing the greatest learning of SPIN should have had a significantly higher productivity gain than the subgroup showing a poorer level of learning.

4. Finally, we compared the performance of both subgroups with a similar-size control group of 52 untrained salespeople to make sure that the changes weren't caused by a market, product, or organizational effect.

Once we'd decided on this methodology, we set about reexamining our data in an attempt to isolate the elusive Hawthorne effect. Our results are shown in Figure A.16, which reveals that there *was* a Hawthorne effect at work but that, as with most Hawthorne effects, its impact was short-lived.

First, let's look at the performance of the subgroup of people higher on SPIN skills. In Figure A.16 their results show an increase *during*

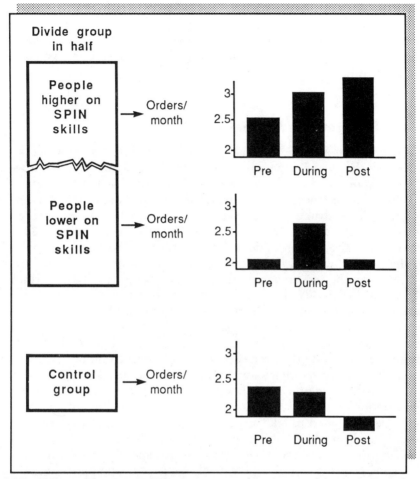

Figure A.16. Isolating the Hawthorne effect.

the training period, when they were receiving the most attention. But, more important, their results continue to improve *after* the training is over, when they are receiving no attention that might create a Hawthorne effect.

In contrast, the results from the subgroup of people lower on SPIN skills show a dramatic improvement *during* the 4-month training period. However, as soon as the training attention is withdrawn, their results slip back to the original level. Here we have the Hawthorne effect—isolated for the first time in the field of sales performance.

Finally, let's look at the control group. Selling the same products in the same difficult capital goods market, their performance shows a decrease both during and after the other group's training. So we can conclude that the improvement of the higher SPIN subgroup did not result from market, product, or organizational factors. Compared with the control group, even the performance of the lower SPIN subgroup looks good. Instead of showing a gradual decline, its people are at least holding their own.

Final Thoughts on Evaluation

There are even more tests I'd like to carry out before I'll be totally satisfied that the ideas I've described in this book will significantly improve the results of major sales. It's a never-ending quest. When I was growing up in Borneo there were no roads and all trips were by river. At any point of any journey, if you asked the boatman how much farther, you'd get the same reply—"Satu tanjong lagi"—which means "One more bend." Evaluation studies are like that. Just when you think you've all the proof you need, there's one more bend.

We'll probably never get round that final bend. But I hope you'll agree that in our search for proof, Huthwaite has explored the river carefully. We've tried to take an objective and critical look at our own models and whether they work—and by doing so we've become better researchers, designers, and trainers. Above all, we've been able to increase the practical effectiveness of our approach. Ironically, by going through these very academic-sounding testing routines, we've improved our understanding of what makes practical good sense, measured by its contribution to sales results. I wish more people in the training business could be persuaded to take a similar approach. It would be very satisfying to us if this book stimulated more research into effective selling. I'd like to think that eventually, through patient investigation and experiment, researchers will be able to take more of the mystery out of the major sale and make it as clearly understandable as any other business function.

Appendix **B**
Closing-Attitude Scale

In Chapter 2 we looked at closing techniques, and in the "Attitude problems" section I mentioned an attitude scale that we developed to measure people's feelings about closing. If you'd like to test yourself, here's how:

1. Read the following 15 statements about closing.

2. After each statement, put a check in the box that most nearly represents your own opinion.

3. Follow the instructions at the end of the scale to calculate and interpret your score.

1. Closing is the most valuable of all techniques for increasing sales.

    5 ☐ Strongly agree

    4 ☐ Agree

    3 ☐ Uncertain

    2 ☐ Disagree

    1 ☐ Strongly disagree

2. Trying to close a sale too often will reduce your changes of success.

    1 ☐ *Strongly agree*

    2 ☐ *Agree*

    3 ☐ *Uncertain*

    4 ☐ *Disagree*

    5 ☐ *Strongly disagree*

3. Unless you know a lot of closing techniques, you will be unable to sell effectively.

    5 ☐ *Strongly agree*

    4 ☐ *Agree*

    3 ☐ *Uncertain*

    2 ☐ *Disagree*

    1 ☐ *Strongly disagree*

4. Even at the start of a sale, it never hurts to use a trial close.

    5 ☐ *Strongly agree*

    4 ☐ *Agree*

    3 ☐ *Uncertain*

    2 ☐ *Disagree*

    1 ☐ *Strongly disagree*

5. Weak closing is the most common cause of lost sales.

    5 ☐ *Strongly agree*

    4 ☐ *Agree*

    3 ☐ *Uncertain*

    2 ☐ *Disagree*

    1 ☐ *Strongly disagree*

6. Customers are less likely to buy if they recognize that you are using closing techniques.

    1 ☐ *Strongly agree*

    2 ☐ *Agree*

    3 ☐ *Uncertain*

    4 ☐ *Disagree*

    5 ☐ *Strongly disagree*

7. You cannot close too often when selling.

    5 ☐ *Strongly agree*

    4 ☐ *Agree*

    3 ☐ *Uncertain*

    2 ☐ *Disagree*

    1 ☐ *Strongly disagree*

8. Closing techniques don't work with professional buyers.

    1 ☐ *Strongly agree*

    2 ☐ *Agree*

    3 ☐ *Uncertain*

    4 ☐ *Disagree*

    5 ☐ *Strongly disagree*

9. The ABC of selling is *Always Be Closing.*

    5 ☐ *Strongly agree*

    4 ☐ *Agree*

    3 ☐ *Uncertain*

    2 ☐ *Disagree*

    1 ☐ *Strongly disagree*

10. It's your other behavior earlier in the sale, not your closing technique, that determines whether a customer will buy.

    1 ☐ *Strongly agree*

    2 ☐ *Agree*

    3 ☐ *Uncertain*

    4 ☐ *Disagree*

    5 ☐ Strongly disagree

11. You should try to close every time that you see a buying signal.

    5 ☐ *Strongly agree*

    4 ☐ *Agree*

    3 ☐ *Uncertain*

    2 ☐ *Disagree*

    1 ☐ *Strongly disagree*

12. From the moment you enter the customer's office, you should act as though the sale has already been made.

    5 ☐ *Strongly agree*

    4 ☐ *Agree*

    3 ☐ *Uncertain*

    2 ☐ *Disagree*

    1 ☐ *Strongly disagree*

13. If a customer resists your trial close, then it's a sign that you should have closed more forcefully.

    5 ☐ *Strongly agree*

    4 ☐ *Agree*

    3 ☐ *Uncertain*

    2 ☐ *Disagree*

    1 ☐ *Strongly disagree*

14. No matter how good your other skills, you will never succeed unless you have good closing techniques.

    5 ☐ *Strongly agree*

    4 ☐ *Agree*

    3 ☐ *Uncertain*

    2 ☐ *Disagree*

    1 ☐ *Strongly disagree*

15. Using closing techniques early in the sale is a sure way to antagonize customers.

    1 ☐ *Strongly agree*

    2 ☐ *Agree*

    3 ☐ *Uncertain*

    4 ☐ *Disagree*

    5 ☐ *Strongly disagree*

Calculate your Score

To calculate your score, take the number (between 1 and 5) of the box that you checked for each statement and add up your total for the 15 statements.

Theoretically, a score of 45 is absolutely neutral. A higher score shows a positive attitude toward closing, and a lower score shows a negative attitude. In practice, most salespeople score a little above 45, and in our studies we allowed for this by taking a score above 50 as demonstrating a favorable attitude toward closing.

What Do the Scores Mean?

In the study described in Chapter 2 (see Figure 2.2), the salespeople with the best results were those with a low (unfavorable) score: one below 50.

As Chapter 2 explains, however, the effectiveness of closing techniques depends on the type of selling you do. If your business involves low-value goods and services, unsophisticated customers, and no after-sale relationship with the customer, then a very favorable attitude toward closing (a score above 50) might well be justified in terms of your selling situation. But if you score above 50 on this test and your business involves larger sales, sophisticated customers, and a continuing post-sale relationship, then please read Chapter 2 very carefully. In the larger sale, closing techniques are more of a liability than an asset.

Index

About the Author

Neil Rackham is president and founder of Huthwaite, Inc. His organization researches, consults, and gives seminars for over 200 leading sales organizations around the world, including Xerox, IBM, AT&T, Kodak, and Citicorp. His academic background is in research psychology. It was at the University of Sheffield, England, that he began his research into sales effectiveness that resulted in SPIN. He is the author of over 50 articles and several books which have been translated into a total of 11 languages.

Refer questions to:

Huthwaite, Inc.
Wheatland Manor
15164 Berlin Turnpike
Purcellville, VA 20132 USA
(540)882-3212 (telephone)
(540)822-9004 (fax)